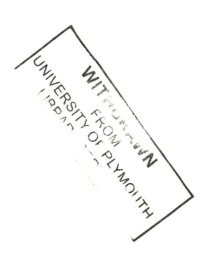

The Political Career
of Oliver St. John,
1637–1649

The Political Career of Oliver St. John, 1637–1649

William Palmer

DELAWARE

Newark: University of Delaware Press
London and Toronto: Associated University Presses

Associated University Presses
440 Forsgate Drive
Cranbury, NJ 08512

Associated University Presses
25 Sicilian Avenue
London WC1A 2QH, England

Associated University Presses
P.O. Box 39, Clarkson Pstl. Stn.
Mississauga, Ontario,
L5J 3X9 Canada

The paper used in this publication meets the requirements of the American National Standard for Permanence of Paper for Printed Library Materials Z39.48-1984.

Library of Congress Cataloging-in-Publication Data

Palmer, William, 1951–
  The political career of Oliver St. John, 1637–1649 / William Palmer.
    p. cm.
  Includes bibliographical references and index.
  ISBN 0-87413-453-6 (alk. paper)
  1. St. John, Oliver, 1598?–1673. 2. Great Britain—History—Civil War, 1642–1649—Biography. 3. Great Britain—Politics and government—1625–1649. 4. Legislators—Great Britain—Biography. 5. Judges—Great Britain—Biography. I. Title.
DA419.S7P35 1993
941.06'092—dc20
[B]   91-51138
                                                                CIP

PRINTED IN THE UNITED STATES OF AMERICA

Contents

Acknowledgments

This book began as a doctoral dissertation at the University of Maine, and many people have contributed to it along the way. In the History Department at the University of Maine, Jack Battick, Bill Baker, Stu Doty, Bill Tebrake, and Anne Bridges provided advice and encouragement during the course of research and writing. After completing the dissertation and receiving my degree in 1981, I became a member of the "lost generation" of Ph.D.s of the late 1970s and 1980s, unable to find a permanent teaching job. The aforementioned group repeatedly urged me not to give up the quest, and two History Department chairs, Dave Smith and Arthur Johnson, enabled me to survive by offering work as an adjunct professor and as a research assistant. Without that assistance, I doubt that I could have continued in academic life.

Through the somewhat extended period of my education and the gloomy times of academic underemployment, my parents, Raymond and Carol Palmer, and my aunts, Edith and Eva Palmer, remained optimistic about my prospects, and, if they doubted that I would ever find permanent employment in academia, they never showed it. At the same time, my parents-in-law, Imogene and the late Lloyd Brightman, allowed me to live in their house, disrupt their lives, and marry their daughter. I learned a great deal from Lloyd, and it is one of my deepest regrets that he did not live to see this work in print. He was very much a part of it, and its publication would have pleased him greatly. I miss him.

In 1984 I was fortunate enough to become a member of the Department of History at Marshall University. In addition to gaining entry into the mysterious world of tenure track, I became a member of a department of conscientious professionals. I am grateful to David Woodward, David Duke, Donna Spindel, and Frances Hensley, for showing, by precept and example, that it is possible to do research while teaching twelve hours a semester, serving on committees, and raising children. I am also grateful to Marshall University for releasing me from teaching one course each spring and providing me with two generous summer research grants. In addition, the National Endowment for the Humanities awarded me a Travel to Collections

Grant in 1988, which enabled me to take a vital research trip at a critical moment in the book's development.

Others provided sound advice rather than economic support. Many of my ideas about Oliver St. John were tried out at conferences and on individuals. I thought that I knew what Oliver St. John was about when I attended the 1980 AHA meeting in Washington. But thirty minutes' conversation with Mark Kishlansky revealed to me that I had far to go. Caroline Hibbard, Martin Havran, Derek Hirst, Rick Stacey, and Mike Young offered advice and criticism on specific points. Rick Stacey allowed me to see his important essay on Strafford's trial in advance of its publication, which led me to begin thinking along altered lines about the events of the spring of 1641. None of the people listed here, of course, is responsible for any of the inadequacies of the book, especially since I did not always heed their counsel. Jennifer McDowell kindly helped with the proofreading.

Archivists and librarians were very helpful to me. Bill Bidwell and David Underdown made my stay at the Yale Center for Parliamentary History a pleasure, and librarians at Marshall cheerfully and efficiently responded to my requests for interlibrary loan materials.

I would like to express my gratitude to several editors for granting permission to reprint materials that were first published in their journals. Part of chapter 2 originally appeared as "Oliver St. John and the Legal Language of Revolution in England, 1640–1642," in *The Historian* 51 (1989): 263–82. A portion of chapter 5 was published as "Oliver St. John and the Middle Group in the Long Parliament, 1643–45: A Reappraisal," in *Albion* 14 (1982): 20–26. And part of chapter 6 is reprinted with permission from *Anglican and Episcopal History/The Historical Magazine of the Protestant Episcopal Church* 52 (1983): 17–27.

Finally, my greatest debt is to my wife, Gretchen. She went to conferences and libraries with me, tolerated the sprawl of books and photocopies that was my corner of the living room, and always supported my research efforts. As Christopher Hill once said about his wife, "She is the last to be thanked, and should always come first." Aaron Palmer, two years old at this writing, contributed nothing to the writing of this book, but every day in a thousand ways he makes his father feel like one of the luckiest men on earth.

The Political Career
of Oliver St. John,
1637–1649

Introduction

Like a small tree in a grove of majestic oaks, Oliver St. John, a pivotal figure in the English Civil War, has suffered a curious neglect. The English Civil War has inspired historians to undertake a thorough and exhaustive assault on the records of practically every aspect of the age. Biographies or studies abound of almost all the major figures of the time, especially of St. John's close associates, Pym and Cromwell.[1] Several new works on Cromwell have already appeared in 1990s, and there have been two books on the career of the younger Vane, and several on John Hampden, one as recent as 1976.[2] In 1979 a new biography of Denzil Holles appeared.[3] Lesser figures, like Henry Marten and Hugh Peter, have also found their Boswells.[4] Even the pompous Bulstrode Whitelocke, perhaps one-quarter as important as he reckoned himself, was the subject of a recent biography.[5] Yet, no biography of St. John exists, and, outside my own work, only one major article has been published about him.[6]

This neglect of St. John is even more astonishing when the role he played in the Great Rebellion is considered. He, Holles, and perhaps Vane were the only men to be vitally involved in the events that spanned the entire decade of the 1640s. Pym and Hampden, doubtless more important in the early stages of the Rebellion, were dead by the end of 1643. Cromwell and Ireton, giants of the later 1640s, were relatively insignificant figures before 1645. St. John may be judged unique in that he was the only man to play equally conspicuous roles in the opposition to Ship Money in 1637, the execution of the earl of Strafford, the signing of the Solemn League and Covenant, the creation of the New Model Army, and the conflict between Parliament and the Army in 1647. In 1649 controversy still swirled around him when he refused to sign King Charles I's death warrant.

St. John's participation in these events, moreover, was not superficial. As forcefully as anyone, he stated the constitutional basis for opposition to the fiscal policies of Charles I in his arguments against Ship Money. This opposition culminated in his dramatic speech on 29 April 1641, calling for the execution of the earl of Strafford, when St. John described "Black Tom" as "vermin" and argued for Parliament's right to remove corrupting influences on the monarchy.[7]

11

The death of Pym transformed St. John from a subordinate figure, whose primary role had been to serve as defender of a perceived ancient constitution, into a practical man of politics, and he moved in the next two years into the power vacuum left by Pym. St. John helped perform the difficult task of luring the Scots into the War without committing Parliament to a Presbyterian Church structure. By subtle means rather than frontal attack, he succeeded where Vane and Marten had failed in dislodging the stodgy earl of Essex from command of the parliamentary armies. The league with the Scots and the removal of Essex laid the groundwork for the establishment of a new and aggressive fighting force, the New Model Army. St. John dexterously guided its passage through the Commons in a series of close divisions. In the end the political skills of St. John would be overshadowed by the military genius of Cromwell. Nevertheless, in his endeavors from 1643 to 1645, St. John helped deliver the military alliance that eventually won the war for Parliament.

The name of Oliver St. John also looms large in recent debates on the origins and course of the English Civil War. During the past decade our understanding of the Civil War era has been greatly transformed by several scholars whose works have been collectively organized under the banner of revisionism. Revisionist scholarship, of course, is not the only trend in recent early Stuart historiography, but it is the one that has generated the most attention and provided the most arresting insights. Although all revisionist scholars do not hold identical views or agree on all questions, the revisionist position, generally speaking, consists of several related clusters of ideas. The English Revolution of 1640–60, if there was one, was not a class struggle originating in the convulsive social changes of previous decades. The outbreak of the Civil War in 1642 should be interpreted primarily as a reaction by county communities against the centralizing tendencies of Charles's government.[8] Nor was Puritanism, strictly speaking, one of the main causes of the Civil War. In the minds of several scholars, the Puritanism of the early seventeenth century was already well integrated into society and had only a minimal revolutionary potential. The ascendancy of Laud and the Arminians, however, transformed Puritanism into a force for revolt.[9] Nor was the Civil War the result of the struggle for sovereignty between king and Parliament. According to several scholars, Parliament was fundamentally a weak body before 1640; it contained no genuine opposition; its members were more influenced by self-interest than by ideology or principle; and the apparent friction of the 1620s was caused by the financial demands of war rather than by constitutional conflicts. The events of the 1620s, moreover, have little connection with the events of the 1640s, and a separate set of causes must be sought for them.[10] Collectively, the various components of revisionism have combined to cast serious doubts on the inevitability of Civil War, or that its outbreak had any long-term social, economic, or ideological causes.[11] Presently, the most active revisionist position, advanced in differing ways by Anthony Fletcher, Caroline Hibbard, and John Morrill, holds that religious issues rather than constitutional issues were preeminent in the minds of members of Parliament between 1640 and 1642. The belief that England was gripped by an insidious Catholic conspiracy, these historians suggest, drove men to resist royal tyranny—not constitutional issues.[12] Revisionism has had its greatest impact on pre-1642 historiography. But Mark Kishlansky has extended aspects of the revisionist position into the Civil War era itself, arguing that "consensus decision making" remained the norm of parliamentary politics as late as 1647.[13]

Revisionist scholarship has been subjected to an often fierce attack, although even its most vituperative critics would concede that revisionism has served as an important corrective to previously determinist modes of explanation.[14] This study of St. John, while not intended as a test case for or against the revisionist position, does, nonetheless, to a certain degree address points raised by both the revisionists and their critics. From one angle St. John was clearly not a politician of limited, local interests. Nor were religious grievances at the forefront of his political agenda. As the primary spokesman of those offended by the king's imposition of Ship Money, he saw issues in broad, constitutional terms, and in 1640–41 he was a persistent voice urging his colleagues in the Commons to connect the Crown's problems in 1640–41 with its actions in the 1630s. On the other hand, in the spring of 1642, as members of Parliament engaged in bitter debates over the militia issue, St. John took little part, and in June 1642 he asked the members of the House of Commons if they thought that he, as the King's solicitor, should go to York to join the King, as he had been ordered, on the raising of the royal standard.[15] St. John was clearly trying to cover himself in the event of a Royalist triumph, but the episode also makes him appear as a man of constitutional principles and as the most reluctant of rebels.

One cannot deny indications of the importance of religion in St. John's career. His education at Cambridge and Lincoln's Inn, his close association with such convinced Puritans as Hampden, Pym, and Cromwell, and his drafting of the Root and Branch Bill suggest that he shared at least some of their interests. His second wife's ardent Puritanism, his commentaries on biblical texts, and a commonplace book in his possession offer further indication that St. John was well schooled in the basic tenets of Elizabethan and early Stuart Puritanism.

But the religious outlook that emerges from a study of St. John becomes too muddied and vague to prove anything conclusive. Outside of his introduction of the Root and Branch Bill, the importance of religion in his life must be discerned from arguing from his connections with others, always a dangerous enterprise in the world of early Stuart history. Even the commonplace book in his possession must be used with caution. It appears to have been compiled by several members of St. John's family, and it is not immediately evident which entries can be attributed directly to him.

On the other hand, there is no mistaking St. John's legalism. His speeches on Ship Money, Strafford, and other matters stake out a clear position. From the Ship Money case through the king's trial and execution, St. John supported measures designed to restrict the powers of the monarchy and remove its most objectionable advisors without substantial reconstruction or revision of the system. St. John's post-Restoration attempt at self-justification, like most similar exercises, should be treated with caution. But it was not without some justice that he claimed in it, "I have in my capacity endeavored constantly to prefer the civil government, in Parliament, and out of Parliament, from the sword and all arbitrary power . . . [and] I always opposed myself, to the taking away or altering of the law . . ."[16]

In a sense the revisionists have replaced previous modes of explanation with a Clarendonlike model. Clarendon believed that St. John's opposition to aspects of royal policy, like that of Pym and several others, derived primarily from personal ambition. Thwarted in their drive to achieve position and influence, St. John and others manipulated Parliament to make compromise impossible. St. John clearly did covet government office, and he clung to his post as solicitor as long as possible. But this work will attempt to establish two essential points about St. John's career. First, as suggested in preceding paragraphs, St. John's opposition derived primarily from fiercely held constitutional principles, and during Strafford's trial and the Militia Bill debates he risked his position to fight for his constitutional principles. Second, as we shall see, he tried repeatedly before 1642 to reach a settlement that would be acceptable to both sides.

Yet, despite his prominent role in critical events of the revolutionary era, St. John continues to languish in relative neglect by historians. Reasons for this neglect, however, are not hard to find. Among political actors, dynamic orators generally attract the most notice. Skillful politicians, who work quietly behind the scenes, seldom receive their due from historians. St. John was an effective but not captivating speaker. He often convinced his audience to take the course of action he desired, but his speeches, especially early in his career, were long and ponderous. His speech on the attainder of the earl of Strafford, for example, took several hours and was crammed with hundreds of references to precedents and statutes from English history. Only on rare occasion could St. John rise above his usual plodding format and exhibit a flair for dramatic delivery or the ability to turn a telling phrase.

Moreover, St. John remains neglected because the evidence about his life is so scarce. For many of the key figures of the Revolution we have at least samplings of their correspondence or an intimate remembrance by someone who knew them well. Others exist on page after page of parliamentary records. These kinds of materials have enabled historians to etch vivid, if caricatured, portraits of several of the men who opposed the King in the 1640s. There is the precise, efficient John Pym, artfully trying to achieve a reasonable financial settlement for the King, while at the same time consumed by the need to save England from what he believed was the blight of popery. There is Oliver Cromwell, master of the later stages of the conflict, bellowing his intention to shoot the King and hang all noblemen. There is Henry Marten, drinking, wenching, and cracking jokes in the midst of events that pained most men very deeply.

No such portrait of St. John is possible. He remains a shadowy figure. Evidence about him is scanty and rarely yields anything definitive. Details about his early life and personal affairs are especially scarce. Even the records of his public business do not reveal as much about him as they do for others. His name does not leap from practically every page of the records as does Pym's. No illuminating four-volume collection of his letters exists as it does for Cromwell. Nor did St. John keep a diary like D'Ewes, compose a history like Clarendon, or write an acerbic memoir like Holles.[17] The historian wishes, as J. M. Thompson once did about Marat, for just thirty minutes of conversation with someone who knew St. John. The most instructive sources about him are the contemporaneously printed copies of his speeches in Parliament on Ship Money, the bishops, and Strafford's attainder. These speeches provide us with a definite idea of the man's political beliefs, but very little about his personal life. The remainder of our information must be culled from the brief and fragmented discussions of his activities by other witnesses, who were often hostile.

The publication of several new sources in which St. John figures prominently, such as two volumes of D'Ewes's diary, Thomas Aston's Short Parliament diary, and John Harington's diary, have made this task easier.[18] But even those contemporaries who wrote about him left rather contradictory impressions. Clarendon described him as "a man reserved, and of a dark and clouded countenance, very proud, conversing with very few, and those men of his own humor and inclination."[19] This description gives the impression of a gloomy and humorless man. Yet, elsewhere, Clarendon says that St. John was "beloved" by Parliament.[20] Robert Baillie called him that "sweet man."[21] And Bulstrode Whitelocke testified that St. John was one of Parliament's favorites.[22] In 1644, *Mercurius Britannicus* described him as "the one that hath lighted his candle at Mr. Pym's flames of zeal and piety and now acts with so much virtue."[23] By 1647, however, John Lilburne called St. John a "covetous catchworm."[24] Elsewhere, he was described as a "corrupt lawyer,"[25] and a "pettifogger for Independency."[26] Finally, Denzil Holles considered St. John, along with Cromwell, "the grand designer of the ruin of these three kingdoms."[27]

These diverse opinions, ranging from veneration to contempt, are usually reserved for people with seemingly duplicitous behavior. Duplicitous is often the best description of St. John's actions. He challenged the legality of Ship Money and repeatedly proclaimed his devotion to the Constitution. Yet, he often manipulated that Constitution to serve his own ends, especially when he advocated the attainder of the earl of Strafford on the flimsiest evidence. He was an outspoken opponent of many aspects of royal policy from 1637 to 1641. However, in 1641 he accepted a post in Charles's court as solicitor general. He lured the Scots into the war on Parliament's side. But he discarded them abruptly when he believed they were no longer of any use. He made promises to the Scots about establishing a Presbyterian Church system in England. Yet, it is clear that he had not the slightest intention of ever doing it. He was a formidable opponent of aspects of royal policy in the 1640s and one of the men most responsible for the king's defeat. At the same time, he was a reluctant rebel, and in 1649, even when under extreme pressure, he refused to sign the king's death warrant or act at his trial.

Not only are there problems with the source materials for St. John's life, the sources for the history of the English Civil War itself are uneven and often suspect. Witnesses at Charles I's execution in 1649 could not agree on the color of his clothes. Sir Simonds D'Ewes would occasionally describe a member of Parliament as a "fiery spirit" one day and an "honest, God-fearing man" the next. Even the accounts of the actual participants are tainted by prejudice. Many of them, like Clarendon, Whitelocke, and Holles, wrote their accounts long after the dust had settled on the events they described, in ignorance or violent emotion, relying on notes made years before or old news sheets. Writing long after the fact, they tended to judge the causes of events by their results, a method that frequently distorted their judgments of men and motivations.[28]

Moreover, the total record of events is not complete. There is no *Congressional Record* for the seventeenth-century English Parliament. The *Commons Journals* often merely list the topics of discussion. They do not identify speakers, except in committee or conference reports, or provide division lists. But when there was a division of the House, two members from each side counted the votes. The *Commons Journals* do provide the names of the tellers and the sides they took. For the most part, however, the shifts and turns in the course of parliamentary politics must be sought from news sheets, diarists and memorialists, and a complete accounting is impossible. A further hindrance to our understanding is that the main participants in the English Revolution lived in London. Men living in the same city, as J. H. Hexter once observed, did not need to write letters to each other when they could meet at Westminster and talk.

Perhaps because of these impediments, modern historians have fared no better than St. John's contemporaries in assessing him. Depictions of him range from "an aggressive radical," to "an eloquent advocate of moderation," to "leader of the middle party," to "leader of the war party," to "former middle grouper."[29] There is some accuracy in each of these descriptions, but any attempt to reduce St. John to one phrase or a couple of adjectives is as difficult as distilling the Great Rebellion itself into one gemlike phrase or sentence. The nature of the Civil War changed constantly, and St. John changed with it.

The English Civil War began as a dispute within the governing classes regarding the extent to which parliamentary authority would be necessary to protect liberty, property, and true religion from the whims of what appeared to many of them to be an arbitrary monarch. All three were important to St. John, but liberty and property for him took precedence over true religion. The Ship Money Case and Strafford's trial were crucial in forming his outlook. In 1637, St. John argued that the king had no right to deprive subjects of liberty and property. In 1640 he argued that the king had illegally used the law to violate the rights of Englishmen. In 1641 he argued that Parliament had the right to remove violators of the Constitution. In effect St. John was recognizing that the legal mechanism revered by most Englishmen had failed to bring Charles I and his advisors to account. St. John did not specifically call for Charles's removal, nor was he ever consciously revolutionary. But he was able to express the extent of parliamentary dissatisfaction with the Crown, and implicitly threaten sterner measures, but without committing himself to an irreversible course of action.

Ship Money and the Strafford case evoked such intensity for St. John because the issues they raised were so firmly embedded in the mainstream of seventeenth-century concepts of liberty. To St. John "liberty" conveyed the right of a man to be secure in holding his property. In his eyes the king's attempt to raise money without parliamentary consent constituted a challenge to the property rights of Englishmen. On many occasions St. John carried his legalism too far. The Strafford case was the most blatant example of St. John's willingness to bend the law to his purpose. But the man who fought for the rights of propertied Englishmen in the Ship Money case at the same time supported taking property from other, less-privileged Englishmen, in the fen drainage schemes. St. John was also certainly wrong during the Short Parliament when, referring to 1629, he questioned the king's historic right to dissolve Parliament. He was wrong, as well, to challenge the right of the bishops to sit in judgment of Strafford during the debate on the bill of attainder in April 1641. As Dr. Thomas Mason has shown recently in his biography of Juxon, the bishops had full right to act in any proceedings resulting in a bill.[30]

These flashes of expediency aside, St. John remains firmly grounded in the legalist, empirical tradition of English thought. The English did not rely on abstract philosophical ideas; they depended on experience, derived from custom and tradition. This reliance was the basis of English liberties, not philosophical speculation. Grounded in this tradition, St. John recognized the rights of propertied men. His view of liberty lacked the universal spirit of the ideas of the French Revolution.

When this conservative, constitutional basis for the Rebellion collapsed in 1646 following the end of the first Civil War, St. John faced the dilemma of the constitutionalist. New and threatening ideas, arguing for the extension of the franchise, equality for all men, and lands held in common, had appeared. In many respects these notions represented a greater threat to property and the Constitution than Charles I. What began in the minds of many members as the relatively straightforward attempt to compel a monarch whom they believed to be arbitrary to serve the Constitution turned into a massive outcry to dismantle society, which probably frightened St. John as much as anyone. John Lilburne, the Leveller, sneered at the Constitution, saying that it was "Parliament that keeps the people from seeking their freedom and liberty."[31]

Yet, St. John survived all the travails of the 1640s. In navigating his way through the traps and snares of the Civil War (and eventually the Commonwealth and Protectorate as well), St. John may be compared to the Abbe Sieyès of the French Revolution, who displayed a similar agility in living through the early days of protest, the National Assembly, the September Massacres, the Terror, and Napoleon. Like Sieyes, who authored the famous pamphlet *Qu' est-ce que le Tiers État?* *(What is the Third Estate?)*, St. John did not possess a set of specific goals, only an imprecise vision of a general political ideal. Perhaps for this reason, St. John, like Sieyes, only survived the Civil War, he never mastered it.[32]

"Every historian," A. J. P. Taylor once remarked, "should write a biography if only to learn how different it is from writing history."[33] What Taylor meant exactly is unclear, but he may have meant that an examination of a particular period through a single person's life inevitably produces a distorted picture. The best that can be hoped for is an approximation, especially when there are so many obstacles to understanding. What follows, then, is an examination of part of one man's life and an attempt to relate that life to a larger event, the English Civil War.

To work on the history of the English Civil War, it is necessary to stand on the shoulders of giants, even if it is not possible to see farther than they. The debt here to the works of Gardiner, Hexter, Hirst, Hibbard, Fletcher, Kishlansky, MacCormack, Underdown, and others is vast. As well, anyone who works on Oliver St. John owes a special debt to Valerie Pearl. In two path-breaking articles, one specifically on St. John, the other devoted partly to him and partly to the group often associated with him, she penetrated through the cloud of mystery that previously shrouded the study of St. John, completely recast our ideas about him, and determined the agenda for future study. Pearl clearly established St. John's critical leadership role after Pym's death in 1643, and confirmed that most of his actions are more properly characterized as moderate rather than radical.[34]

Through the efforts of Pearl and many others, most of the key facts regarding St. John's life have been uncovered. Most of the details about his life will be known to some historian somewhere. Still, the way these facts have been selected and ordered will clash with other interpretations of the period. If the ideas of several historians have been questioned in this work, it is not because their virtues have not been recognized, or their works not deeply respected. Clearly, without the works of Pearl and others, this study would be greatly impoverished.

1

Theme and Variations: St. John's Early Career and the Ship Money Case

The early career of Oliver St. John was marked by both tempestuous incidents and mundane events common in the career of a young lawyer. St. John was probably born in 1598, the son of Oliver St. John of Cayshoe, Bedfordshire, and Sarah, daughter of Edward Berkeley of Odell, Bedfordshire. St. John was also the grandson of Oliver St. John of Blethso, the first earl of Bolingbroke. His birth assured him of a desirable social position, but his family was not particularly wealthy.[1] Evidence of his early life is scanty. The first recorded details of his life concerned his education. He entered Queen's College, Cambridge, in 1615 and Lincoln's Inn in 1619. Both institutions had a distinctly Puritan flavor, although it cannot be stated with certainty that St. John was influenced by his experiences at either place. St. John studied at Queen's under John Preston, one of the leading Puritans of the early Stuart era.[2] Moreover, during the 1620s, Lincoln's Inn was a bastion of Puritanism. During St. John's stay the Inn was also attended by a number of other men who would later acquire national prominence. The foremost of these men was William Prynne, an acerbic critic of Laudian innovation. Other men of coming repute who attended Lincoln's Inn at this time included William Noy, William Hakewill, John Glynn, and William Lenthall.[3]

St. John was called to the bar in 1626. By 1629 he was being retained as a lawyer for the Russell family, the earls of Bedford, and he had married advantageously. St. John's bride was the niece of Sir Thomas Barrington, a wealthy Essex gentleman.[4] St. John also became involved in political controversy. In 1629 he was imprisoned briefly for sending his patron, Bedford, a "design of sedition."[5] The charges were dropped eventually, but not before St. John had been brought before Star Chamber.[6] Writing many years later, Clarendon asserted that the episode had a profound effect on St. John. Clarendon stated that St. John "Never forgave the Court the first assault and contracted an implacable displeasure against the Church purely from the company he kept."[7]

The company St. John kept is revealed by his connection with the Providence Island Company. Clarendon believed that St. John and his partner in the alleged sedition, the earl of Bedford, had by this time established an "intimate trust."[8] Bedford was also the parliamentary patron of John Pym, who, in turn, engineered St. John's admission to the Providence Island Company in 1630.[9] St. John's membership in the company may have exercised a powerful influence on his later career. Membership included almost every significant member of the "opposition" to Charles I. The most frequent opponents of the Crown in the House of Lords, the earls of Warwick and Bedford and Lord Say and Sele, were members. Included from the Commons were John Pym, Benjamin Rudyerd, Sir Thomas Barrington, Gilbert Gerrard, and John Hampden, all of whom either had been conspicuous opponents of the Crown in the 1620s or would become so in the 1640s.

The Providence Island Company venture had been initiated by the earl of Warwick in 1628 or 1629.[10] Subscriptions for membership were invited in the summer of 1630, and by autumn the company was complete.[11] Its first recorded meeting took place 19 November 1630, and £200 was the sum required of the initial investors. Few of them, however, made the full payment, not even the wealthiest ones, like Warwick and Rudyerd. Oliver St. John was also not prepared to make the full payment at this first meeting. In the minutes of the meeting the recorder noted, "Mr. St. John of Lincoln's Inn was allowed to participate, though he was not able to put down a single pound."[12] The recorder also noted that John Robartes and John Graunt, along with St. John, had also been induced to join the company under Pym's influence.[13]

St. John's acceptance into the ranks of the Providence Island Company signals that he had already acquired some degree of status among men of power and wealth. St. John appears to have taken no part in the financial direction of the company. Rather, his role in the company was to provide legal counsel.[14]

There are only three other indications of St. John's financial situation. All three suggest, as does his inability to put down any money at the first meeting of Providence Island Company, the likelihood that he was a man of modest, rather than considerable means. The first evidence of his financial situation was his marriage. The earl of Bedford had interceded with the Barrington family to arrange the match. The Barringtons were apparently reluctant to approve the match because St. John's estate was so small. Thomas Barrington placed it at at £200 in 1629.[15] The second example of St. John's wealth is a record of a land purchase in Huntingdonshire by St. John, jointly with several men who lent him the money for the purchase in 1635. Neither the price nor the amount of land is recorded, however.[16]

The third example is St. John's involvement in the draining of the fens, a scheme promoted by the Crown and others to transform supposedly barren and unprofitable fen lands into productive, arable farmland. This project was a favored enterprise of the earl of Bedford. Fen draining threatened the rights and livelihoods of the inhabitants of approximately 1,430 square miles of lands in eastern England. It was vigorously opposed by many in the targeted areas—including Sir Thomas Steward, a self-proclaimed representative of the fen dwellers, who claimed that drainage would unfairly disrupt the lives of the people who lived there.[17] The drainage schemes were essentially an intrusion in local affairs by courtiers and entrepreneurs facilitated by Charles's encouragement. In 1634 the Crown interceded on the side of the investors to allow the project to proceed. The reason for the Crown's intercession was that the investors agreed to cede to the Crown 12,000 of the 107,000 acres they purchased.[18] The drainage was completed in 1637, and the land was distributed to the shareholders, one of whom was Oliver St. John. Again, neither the amount of his investment nor the extent of his holdings is known.[19]

This sort of incomplete evidence makes speculation on St. John's financial condition perilous. Key facts are missing from his recorded ventures, and there is no way of knowing how many of his dealings went unrecorded. The enterprises with which he was connected also disclose very little. St. John committed himself to projects that involved both men of vast incomes, like Bedford, and men of limited resources, like Cromwell. In any case, none of his ventures appears to have been particularly profitable.[20] St. John clearly was not a wealthy man, nor did he become so through investment. Nevertheless, by his investments, successful or not, St. John was a participant in enterprises in the mainstream of seventeenth-century economic life.

Thus, by 1637, Oliver St. John had established a limited but estimable reputation for himself. His duties for the earl of Bedford and the Providence Island Company suggest that his legal acumen already commanded respect. And his marriage, his connection with Bedford, and his membership in the Providence Island Company also placed him squarely amid men of power and who had opposed royal policy in the 1620s and would oppose it again in the 1630s and 1640s. St. John's reputation, then, among men of power and prestige, was promising in 1637. But he had yet to make a national impact. Such an influence would be achieved by his role in the Ship Money case of 1637.

Ship Money was basically a traditional means of financing the construction of the royal fleet. Each county bordering on the sea and the inland ports, such as London, contributed one or more ships, fully equipped and manned. They also retained the option of making a money payment in lieu of providing a ship, according to a scale based on an assessment of the county's wealth. At this point each sheriff broke down the assessment into smaller portions payable by the boroughs and individual property owners, proportionate to their land and wealth. Ship Money had been levied frequently in the past, although it was seldom exacted without protest. Even in the year of the Armada, the call for ships met with fierce opposition.[21] As late as 1628 the Crown had withdrawn the imposition when the inhabitants of the county of Buckinghamshire objected bitterly.[22]

The discord over Ship Money was prompted by several considerations. The first issue of contention was that Ship Money was collected without consulting Parliament. Equally divisive was the conflict between the towns and counties, especially between the coastal and inland districts.[23] Coastal communities resented bearing the heaviest burden for defense. But the inland communities were inclined to regard the distant crisis as the problem of a particular locality. When that crisis became a national issue, they considered it the Crown's responsibility.[24]

The difficulties of Charles I's government only exacerbated those antagonisms. Since the dissolution of Parliament in 1629, Charles had attempted to live off his own devices, avoiding Parliament.[25] The phrase "Eleven Years' Tyranny" has often been applied to the period between 1629 and 1640. But there was nothing inherently tyrannical about a king ruling without Parliament. The Estates General in France had been dissolved since 1614, and for all practical purposes there was no parliamentary government in England between 1610 and 1621, either. It makes more sense to regard the period between 1629 and 1640 as one of Charles's Personal Rule. In many respects Charles managed the business of government more effectively and with less aggravation by himself than he had with Parliament.[26]

This situation does not mean, of course, that the period of Charles's Personal Rule did not pose its own problems. Repeatedly, Charles and his principal advisor, Attorney General William Noy, seized on the implementation of obscure, long unenforced, and obsolete laws and statutes, to raise money. The devices employed by Charles and Noy were often technically legal, but by their obscurity and borderline legality they tended to foster projects that were found to offend someone. Trade duties remained the most useful levy, but an old tax on farm products was reinstated. Other methods included increasing knights' fees and the penalties for nonpayment, rigidly enforcing the forest laws, some instituted as far back as the Conquest, and widening the role of the Court of Wards. All these devices were, as noted, perfectly legal, time-honored means of raising money. They had been intended, however, as temporary expedients, not permanent institutions.

The revival of the Ship Money tax in 1634 was another scheme to avoid summoning Parliament. It was also somewhat different from the other impositions. Precedent required the presence of a threat to the safety of the realm before Ship Money could be collected. In 1634 the king could not cite any declared enemies. There was, however, the continuing menace of Dunkirk privateers in the Channel, who disrupted English shipping, and the Barbary corsairs, who had landed in 1634 on the coast of Cornwall and had captured thirty Englishmen, whom they quickly sold into slavery.[27]

After the corsair raid the first writs for Ship Money were sent to the sheriffs of the coastal communities in October 1634. From this writ the Crown raised about £40,000 for the Navy.[28] In August 1635 the Privy Council issued writs for extending the collection of Ship Money to the inland counties. By 1 March the king had commanded the county of Buckinghamshire to provide, at Portsmouth, a 450-ton ship, complete with officers, 110 skilled and experienced mariners, and a sufficient quantity of arms for war. If the county preferred, a cash payment could be substituted.

Peers as well as commoners opposed the extension of Ship Money to the inland shires. The question of parliamentary assent arose almost immediately. In an emotional letter, Lord Danby implored the king to vote the money in Parliament rather than raise it in this fashion.[29] When the king summoned the earl of Warwick to ask him if he had opposed Ship Money in Essex, Warwick openly admitted it, justifying his opposition on the grounds that Parliament would grant any necessary funds for a war against Catholic powers.[30]

To fortify his position in the midst of mounting opposition, the king sought an opinion of judges on the legality of Ship Money and the range of the King's rights in defending his kingdom in times of danger.[31] The phrasing of the questions in terms of national defense fairly dictated the judges' response. They held that, in respect to threats, such as piracy or invasion, Ship Money might be levied on the ports and maritime counties. Furthermore, they decreed that when the safety of the realm was at stake the whole kingdom should bear the cost. In February 1637 a second opinion affirmed the King's right, indeed his obligation, to determine the existence of a national danger and act on it.[32]

Opponents of Ship Money also decided to seek legal redress. A wealthy Buckinghamshire gentleman, John Hampden, sought to test the legality of Ship Money by refusing to pay his £20 assessment.[33] Money was not the issue. A man of great wealth, Hampden could easily have paid the levy against him. This fact suggests the possibility that Hampden's decision to challenge the Crown was facilitated by his membership in the Providence Island Company. Several of the members of the company comprised a formidable bloc of opposition to Ship Money. Pym, Barrington, and the earl of Warwick all spoke publicly against it. Lord Say also refused to pay.[34] And Oliver St. John was chosen to plead the case. At any rate, whether Hampden acted on his own initiative or was spurred on by others, he was in a sound position to oppose Ship Money. An exemplary man, neither a habitual grumbler against the Crown nor an excitable Puritan, Hampden brought a legitimacy to the case that made it appear that his opposition was based on logic and sincerity.

The selection of Oliver St. John to defend Hampden indicates that St. John's legal abilities were already held in the highest esteem. Even the Crown considered St. John a man to be respected. Before the trial commenced, St. John's rooms were searched by William Beecher, a clerk of the King's Council, with a warrant provided by the Council in June 1637. The search was conducted, one contemporary surmised, because of St. John's retention as Hampden's lawyer and because "he had been a diligent searcher of records concerning forest bounds and laws."[35] The actual findings of the search are not known, but a week later another reason for the search was proposed. A second anonymous author believed that the Council suspected St. John of assisting Henry Burton in his litigation against the Crown.[36] Burton was on trial for his opposition to episcopacy and his labeling of all bishops as "upstart mushrooms." The arguments he used in his defense apparently were considered by the Crown to be too sophisticated for a layman to assemble without the assistance of a lawyer, and the Crown presumed St. John to be that lawyer.[37] Despite this theorizing, the collaboration with Burton was never established. In any case St. John willingly acquiesced in the search, bundling his papers together for Beecher, but denying any connection with Burton. His papers were returned two or three days later, but they revealed no conclusive evidence.[38]

St. John undertook the Ship Money case, undoubtedly aware of several thorny problems. He and the other counsel for the defense,

Robert Holborne, knew in advance that the court had already rendered two favorable opinions on Ship Money. Even more challenging, perhaps, they would be obliged to avoid political considerations. The protests against Ship Money arose from an undercurrent of dissatisfaction, sometimes economic, sometimes political. It would be perhaps easier to demonstrate that Charles was being unfair politically rather than legally wrong, but this kind of argument would not serve their purpose.[39] St. John and Holborne recognized that they would have to urge purely legal objections, based on precedent and tradition, rather than emotion or expediency. Moreover, they knew that the judges had already awarded the king powers of vast dimension in the collection of Ship Money.

St. John therefore commenced his defense by making a substantial concession. Pleading before the Court of the Exchequer, he granted at the outset the right of the king to be the sole judge of the existence of danger. "In this business of defense," he declared, "the *Supreme Protestas* is inherent in his majesty as part of his crown and kingly dignity."[40] This point, he continued, was not in dispute. The real question, claimed St. John, was the manner by which he was to exercise his power. In St. John's view, the king was not entitled to set fines or deliver judgments, except through the judges; thus, he was not empowered to raise money beyond his ordinary revenues, except by Parliament. There were legitimate reasons for this restriction. A representative assembly was most qualified to guard the rights of liberty and property. The King's powers were vast and necessary; they were not limitless. If he was allowed to lay whatever charge he desired on his subjects, St. John declared, it would come to pass that, if the subject possessed anything at all, he was not beholden to the law for it, but his property was left entirely to the "goodness and mercy of the King."[41] With this assertion, St. John stated the argument most basic to the case against Ship Money. By enabling the king to impose taxes without parliamentary consent, the writs of Ship Money threatened the foundation of property itself, a condition few seventeenth-century Englishmen could be expected to countenance.[42]

Dense legal idiom removed, the remainder of St. John's arguments were essentially variations on this theme. In one form or another he simply hammered over and over at the theme that Ship Money posed a serious threat to property rights. He contended that there was no conflict of property and prerogative if a danger arrived so rapidly that application to Parliament was precluded. Certainly, in such cases the king should act according to his own wisdom. The rights of property would merely be in abeyance.[43] In the present case, however, no such danger existed. Writs had been issued in August to equip a fleet, which, admittedly, was not needed until March.[44] What possible reason, asked St. John, could explain not summoning Parliament in the intervening seven months?

St. John, not surprisingly, did not allude to the probable reason. Once summoned, a Parliament might want to discuss other matters, and, in 1637, these matters would very likely include ecclesiastical grievances, of which there were many.[45] And, of course, submerged like a giant iceberg beneath the surface of St. John's arguments was the suspicion that Ship Money was intended as another device to secure the king's permanent independence from Parliament.

St. John supported his position, which took nearly two days to present, with a prodigious amount of antiquarian learning. The bulk of his citations was selected to demonstrate that the kings of England had frequently paid for the services performed in defense of the realm, even when they had been compelled to borrow money to do so.[46]

One last argument proposed by St. John deserves comment. In it St. John replied directly to the Crown's claim that the King was in the best position to act for the general welfare. "In his majesty," St. John concluded, "there is a double capacity, natural and politic. All his prerogatives are . . . to be employed for the common good."[47] Again, the king was entitled to vast and far-ranging powers; but his personal prerogative must be subordinated to the common good.[48]

Like Byron, St. John awoke the day after his speech to find himself famous. He and the other disputants had reviewed the entire course of English history.[49] His arguments largely reaffirmed what other opponents of the Crown had claimed previously. His contribution, however, lay in the clarity, erudition, and skill with which he attacked the property issue. For St. John the Ship Money case could be reduced to one point: the king simply was not allowed by law to take property from a subject without consent. St. John did not advocate resistance as a recourse open to a subject whose property rights have been infringed on. No doubt in 1637 St. John considered that the proper recourse for the aggrieved subject was the law.

This insistence on the sanctity of property and precedent placed St. John squarely in the tradition of Sir Edward Coke as a defender of an imagined Ancient Constitution.[50] St. John shared with Coke the belief that the Constitution was an immemorial part of the English heritage, dating back to the Anglo-Saxon kings, and envisaging a harmonious balance between ruler and ruled. The existence of precedent was vital. Both St. John and Coke believed that a law's antiquity made it binding. Proof that a law or tradition had once been accepted or practiced was adequate reason in their eyes for continuing it.

This fascination with history and legal precedent also reveals the insularity of common lawyers like Coke and St. John. They cited primarily English history and English law, appearing largely indifferent to or ignorant of continental thought or precedent.[51] In summary, St. John was like Coke in that he was conservative in his approach to the Constitution. Neither he nor Coke urged much alteration of government. Their arguments revered tradition and were predicated on the assumption that institutions—especially those like the common law—which have survived, must be presumed to have done so because of their resiliency and value in solving problems that the citizens of the present age could not even conceive, much less solve.[52]

St. John's arguments in the Ship Money case were not unchallenged. The case for the Crown was presented by Solicitor General Edward Littleton and Attorney General Sir John Bankes. Littleton, considered a man of integrity by partisans on both sides, did not try to argue that the king was absolute and that there was no fundamental law other than the King's word. Rather, he asserted, there was a fundamental law, including both King and Parliament, and the king was asking only to be accorded the full measure of his prerogative under that law.[53] In an exposition lasting four days, Littleton embellished and amplified this point.[54] In this exposition he combined his points of law with numerous examples of the dangers already suffered and likely to be suffered in the future at the hands of the Barbary pirates, who infested the seas. There could be grave dangers, he pointed out in answer to St. John's argument, without a declaration of war.[55] This answer was true, of course, but it did not explain why the pirates, who were a perpetual annoyance to English shipping, suddenly required instant attention.

Littleton concluded with a vigorous reassertion of the doctrine of necessity. He acknowledged that the King had no constitutional right to impose Ship Money, except in times of danger. In these times the monarch may be permitted to go beyond the normal course of the law. In times of absolute necessity, moreover, it was impossible to appeal to Parliament. Forty days had to elapse after the issue of writs before Parliament could meet. And, even after Parliament was summoned, both houses commonly spent two or three weeks in conferences. Before the issue could be discussed and an agreement reached, the kingdom could be lost. Clearly, the interest of national security demanded entrusting decisions of this nature to a strong but impartial power. And, clearly, the King was best suited for this role.[56]

The trial closed with the arguments of Holborne on behalf of Hampden, and Attorney General Bankes for the Crown. While both began by following lines of thought already delineated, both departed at key junctures from the arguments previously essayed. For example, whereas St. John allowed that only the King had the power to determine a national emergency, Holborne refused to acknowledge this point and denied that the King ever had a right to tax subjects without their consent.[57]

The speech of Attorney General Bankes is best characterized by his obstinate refusal to concede anything to his opponents. Both St. John and Littleton had granted a certain merit to their adversary's positions. But Bankes flatly rejected even the notion that the court was entitled to inquire into the circumstances under which the king claimed necessity in the Ship Money case. It should suffice to know only that the King desired it. Such power was inherent in the office of King of England and could not be rescinded.[58]

At the completion of the arguments, it was clear, despite the ponderous length of the speeches and the dense mass of precedents, that fundamental differences had been exposed. St. John and Holborne stood resolutely for the rights of the propertied citizens, guaranteed by the Ancient Constitution. Acceptance of the Crown's view, at least that stated by Bankes, however, rendered the Constitution obsolete and meaningless. If Bankes reflected the views of the Crown, the King seemingly rejected a paradigm embraced by most seventeenth-century commentators—one that revered the triumphs commonly associated with the councils of the earliest Anglo-Saxons kings, the Witan, the Great Charter, the Provisions of Oxford, and fourteenth-century resistance to arbitrary rule.[59]

Despite all the passion inspired by the proceedings, they also possessed a certain bloodless quality. They were confined to legal considerations, and the learned counsels for both sides pleaded with reserve. The arguments presented contained no moral or political indignation. As C. V. Wedgwood has written, "The four, honest, painful, learned men resembled for the greater part of the time nothing so much as a group of earnest archaeologists, sieving with assiduity and without passion the dust of the past and selecting this or that recognizable fragment to prove their point".[60]

The decision of the judges was not quickly forthcoming. The case had been heard by the four barons of the Exchequer, as the four judges of that court were called. Perhaps owing to the complexity and seriousness of the case, they quickly postponed judgment to the ensuing term. But the postponement was also very likely obtained for political reasons.[61] Sir Humphrey Davenport, the chief baron of the Exchequer, was in a difficult position. He was a convinced supporter of the king and firmly believed in Charles's right to the money. But during the deliberations he had discerned a technical error in the writ sent to Hampden. This error, he felt, obliged him to pronounce in Hampden's favor. From discussion with his three colleagues he may have gathered that, while two of them were staunch king's men, the last judge, Sir John Denham, had not only observed the technical error but was also wavering on the legality of Ship Money. A two-to-two division would be, in effect, a defeat for the Crown. Thus, to avoid a defeat, Davenport probably arranged for postponement, which would lay the case before all twelve common law judges.[62]

The following spring, then, the judges began to return their opinions on the Hampden case. The first three pronounced decidedly in the king's favor. Their position was summarized by Sir Robert Berkeley, who explained that "the law knows no king yoking policy . . . the people of mere duty are bound to yield unto the King."[63] No conflict between the King and the law, therefore, is even imaginable. Simply put, Berkeley argued, "Rex is lex"; the King is law, and the guardian of his subjects' freedom.

In April two others judges, Sir George Croke and Sir Richard Hutton, found against the king. Their decision was not unexpected. Both men had always doubted the legality of Ship Money. Croke's finding prompted the anonymous comment, "The King has got Ship Money by hook, but not by Croke." Two other judges, Sir John Bramston and Davenport, found for Hampden on the technical grounds described earlier, but they firmly upheld the legality of Ship Money.[64]

The pronouncements of Sir William Jones and Sir John Finch in favor of the King revealed a final tally of seven judges finding for the king and five for Hampden—the most slender majority possible.[65] Chief Justice Finch, however, not only found for the king but returned the most uncompromising opinion. Finch maintained that in every state some man or body of men must exist in authority over others, although this authority is subject to various checks and balances. This power naturally is conceded to the king and entitles him in cases of supreme emergency to brush aside these checks and balances without appeal. Within the purview of this power is his right to void any act of Parliament in the interest of defending the kingdom. In fact, no acts of Parliament intending to bind the king in any way "make any difference."[66]

Historians have placed many interpretations on the Ship Money case. S. R. Gardiner thought that Ship Money brought into focus "all the political dissatisfaction which existed in England."[67] Other historians have stressed the conservatism of the opponents of Ship Money and the meager intellectual content of pre–Civil War political thought.[68] More recently, historians have viewed Ship Money as a provincial problem, a conflict between inland and coastal communities.[69] There are elements of truth in all three points of view. Ship Money did reflect both national political grievances and local tensions in the communities. And, as noted earlier, there are profound currents of conservatism in the thought of even the opponents of Ship Money. But, as a tax, Ship Money appears to have been quite successful. Only a few individuals actually refused to pay, and almost all of the tax levied was collected between 1634 and 1638. Charles asked for less money in 1639, but it was not until 1640 that there was widespread refusal to pay.[70]

Whether conservative or innovative, however, the ideas debated in the Ship Money case found passionate supporters on both sides. The opposition was not silenced by the judges' decision for the king. In fact, wrote Clarendon, Finch's speech "made Ship Money much more abhorred and formidable than all the commitments by the Council table and all the distresses taken by the shrieves of England."[71] Warwick, Saye, and Pym all contemplated emigration to America. On the other hand, those most tightly bound to the Crown did not doubt the immensity of the threat posed by opposition to Ship Money. Archbishop Laud and Chief Justice Finch were convinced that the purpose of Hampden and his friend was "to raise a sedition" because they "were great incendiaries."[72] And on his return from Ireland, one of the king's closest advisors, Thomas Lord Wentworth, wrote, "Hampden and his like ought to be whipped home into right senses."[73]

Opponents also described the case in grandiose terms. Ship Money, said Pym, was "a grievance all are grieved at."[74] Bulstrode Whitelocke declared the whole affair to be "extrajudicially unusual, and of very ill consequence."[75] Sir Symonds D'Ewes believed (albeit privately) that Ship Money was absolutely against the law and an utter oppression of a subject's liberty."[76]

In any case, one certain result is that Oliver St. John emerged, along with Hampden, as a spokesman for those opposed to aspects of Charles's Personal Rule. In the best tradition of Coke and the Ancient Constitution, St. John eloquently upheld the rights of Englishmen to liberty and property. It would be vastly premature, however, to describe St. John as a revolutionary, or to suggest that he was already irrevocably committed to further resistance to the Crown.

A number of things, then, are evident from St. John's early life. It seems clear that he was a man of some personal charm. He established early in his professional life, and with apparent ease, friendship with both men of power and wealth, like Pym and Bedford, and men of a more-common stamp, like Cromwell. He was not a man of wealth, but he was making a concerted effort to wedge his way into a higher level of society through business ventures. Nor was he a man of the people. In the effort to exploit the fens, St. John had been willing to disrupt the lives of a considerable number of people to turn a profit. It is clear as well that St. John was a learned man with a deserved reputation for legal skill. It is not unrealistic to describe him, along with Selden, as among the foremost common lawyers of their time. Moreover, in grappling with the problems posed by Ship Money, St. John refined a theory of government based on the Ancient Constitution and the common law. In the coming years he would go beyond the limits he established in 1637. The position reached by St. John in 1641 or 1645 would be more radical, but still recognizable, from the position he held in 1637.

2

Coming of Age in the Short and Long Parliaments

In 1638, Ship Money was only one of many complex problems confronting Charles I. Despite the fact that the constitutional arguments employed in the Ship Money case raised serious questions about where the fundamental authority in government rested, several other issues appeared more persistent and divisive. Foremost in the minds of many observers were the vexing problems of religion. In 1633, William Laud, promoted to archbishop of Canterbury on the death of George Abbot, launched a campaign to reverse several critical components of the Reformation and restore to the Church its former authority and respect.[1] As early as 1625, Laud had voiced his conviction that the Church reforms demanded by Puritans served to mask a deeper conspiracy against both Church and State and that Puritanism constituted a far more ominous threat to national security than Catholicism. Moreover, Laud maintained an exalted view of his own ecclesiastical authority, conceiving himself to be answerable only to God. Laud's plans for the reconstruction of the Anglican Church consisted of recovering the political power and prestige of the bishops, diminished by several decades of Puritan attacks, restricting lay authority and preaching, dignifying the Anglican liturgy, and rigidly enforcing conformity. These "innovations" were regarded with anger and suspicion by English Puritans, who considered them to be merely subtle ways of reintroducing Catholicism to England. The efforts to "dignify" the liturgy especially were regarded by Puritans as more evidence of Laud's "Popish" tendencies. They were particularly troubling because English Puritans, unlike Laud, deemed Catholicism the real enemy of the realm.

Laud enforced his doctrines tenaciously, harassing or persecuting those who resisted him. Thousands fled to the New World. But, while Laud may have silenced or discouraged many of his critics, in the long run his policy failed. Opposition hardened. Not everyone with an ecclesiastical grievance fled. Even more, perhaps, stayed home and nursed their complaints, dreaming of the coming day of deliverance. Historians of such divergent viewpoints as Lawrence Stone and John Morrill agree on the divisive impact of Laudianism. As Stone commented in 1972, "Laud may justly be regarded as the most important single contributor to the cause of Puritanism in the early seventeenth century." In 1984, Morrill remarked that it is "impossible to underestimate the damage done by the Laudians."[2]

The new directions in Church policy compounded Charles's problems in dealing with his Scottish subjects. Trying to govern Scotland from London posed difficulties even in the best of times. James I, well versed in the nuances and subtleties of Scottish politics, enjoyed a modest success. But ruling Scotland was almost impossible for Charles, who was ignorant of its intricacies and shadings. Ignorance of Scottish hostility toward the Church of England may have led Charles to ask Laud to accompany him to Scotland in 1633. Laud's presence aroused Scottish suspicions that Charles was planning to tamper with their religion. In October 1634, Charles and Laud accepted the contention of the Scottish bishops that the English Book of Common Prayer could not be imposed in Scotland without resistance. Charles and Laud decided instead to instruct the bishops to compose a new liturgy and assemble a new book of canons, conforming as closely as possible to English practice. The task of composition was completed about two years later, and the canons appeared in January 1636. The relatively mild public reception of them encouraged Charles and Laud to proceed with the imposition of the service book in the summer of 1637.[3]

The immediate reaction in Scotland was angry and sustained. Protest began in Edinburgh and spread across the country. The General Assembly of the Church of Scotland undertook the leadership of a national rebellion, and Charles was forced to mobilize an army for the reconquest of Scotland. The English Army, however, failed miserably. Lack of money was a significant, but not completely compelling, explanation. Localism and lethargy in the counties contributed greatly, as public confidence in the venture was almost nonexistent. Many English Puritans, not altogether surprisingly, favored the Scots. Especially debilitating for the military effort was the incompetence of its leaders, who kept the English Army poorly supplied, poorly trained, and poorly led in battle. On the other hand, the Scots were combative and determined, their regiments highly drilled and polished. Able leadership was supplied by Alexander Leslie, a veteran of the continental wars. In 1639, with the English army soundly beaten, peace negotiations began, culminating with the Treaty of Berwick in June 1639.

At this point one of the king's closest advisors, Thomas Wentworth, soon to be earl of Strafford, was recalled from Ireland. Strafford's reputation had been forged by his efficient but uncompromising rule in Ireland.[4] The absolutist techniques employed by Strafford in Ireland, however, did not inspire confidence among the English that he could solve Charles's problems in Scotland, and his ascendency was not widely welcomed. Charles, however, believed that his situation was desperate and regarded Strafford as the only man resourceful enough to save him. The main problem of government was money. The cost of the war and the reparations demanded by the Scottish leaders at Berwick placed the government on the verge of financial collapse. Denied financial aid by the city of London, Strafford concluded that the only way to raise the necessary funds was to summon Parliament, which he advised Charles to do.

It is against this background that the second stage in the political career of Oliver St. John must be understood. As noted earlier, his performance in the Ship Money case had elevated him to national prominence. There had also been significant developments in his personal life. We know that, by 1629, St. John had married Joanna Altham, by whom he had four children, and we know that, by 1639, he had married again. But we do not know the reason for the end of his first marriage nor the name of his second wife. The only surviving evidence concerning her is a letter written to her in October 1638, from her distant cousin, Oliver Cromwell (St. John's wives were both distant cousins of Cromwell).[5] The letter was quite remarkable mainly for what it revealed about Cromwell, and very little of it concerned St. John or his bride. The letter does provide evidence, however, that the second Mrs. St. John and Cromwell were close friends, because Cromwell in the letter joyously described his religious conversion.[6] Cromwell began by acknowledging Mrs. St. John's previous correspondence with him: "I thankfully acknowledge your love in kind remembrance of me upon this opportunity. Alas, you do too highly prize my lines and my company. I may be ashamed to your own expression, considering how unprofitable I am, and the mean improvement of my talent."[7] Cromwell continued by fervently describing his religious rebirth:

Truly no poor creature hath more cause to put forth himself in the cause of his God than I. I have had plentiful wages beforehand and . . . the Lord accepts me in His Son, and gives me to walk in the light. He it is that enlightenth our blackness our darkness. I dare not say He hideth His Face from me. He giveth me to see light in His Light. One beam in a dark hath exceeding much refreshment in it. Blessed be His Name for shining upon so dark a heart as mine! You know what manner of life mine has been. Oh, I lived and loved darkness and hated the light. I was a chief, the chief of sinners. This is true. I hated godliness, yet God had mercy on me. O the riches of His mercy! Praise Him for me, pray for me that he who hath begun a good work would perfect it to the day of Christ.[8]

Cromwell concluded with an expression of love for Mrs. St. John's family. He then jokingly claimed that Oliver St. John was not a man of his word. St. John had promised to write Cromwell about a Mr. Warth of Epping, and Cromwell had not yet received the letter.[9] The exultant tone of the letter suggests that Cromwell was particularly close to Mrs. St. John and that she may have assisted in his religious enlightenment. He seemed to be especially eager to impress her with the depth and sincerity of his conversion. But he expressed no interest in instructing her (or St. John himself) in his new faith, in all like-lihood because she already had embraced it. So it seems fairly clear that St. John's second wife was an ardent Puritan.

St. John's one recorded legal undertaking for the Providence Island Company also occurred in 1638, the year of Cromwell's letter. Since its inception, the company had been trying to settle Tortuga. In 1635, however, after a Spanish raid on the island, the company abandoned its plan and decided to use the island merely as a privateering base.[10] Captain Philip Bell, acting governor of the Tortuga, who had labored diligently for five years to improve conditions for settlement on the island, protested the action and asked to be relieved. The company responded with a curt, tactless letter relieving him of his respon-sibilities and expressing almost no appreciation of his sacrifices on the company's behalf. Bell then demanded that the company compensate him for his labors, which, he contended, should have been performed by the servants promised him as a salary. He alleged that he had received some twenty-five fewer than the company had promised him, and many of them had run away or proved useless. Beyond that, he had cleared a great deal of land to grow crops and therefore absorbed a further loss when the servants did not arrive. All told, he asked for £1,250 from the company, but he acknowledged his willingness to write off £400 that he owed to the company for store goods, tobacco, and bills discharged for him in England.[11]

The company replied that its only contractual obligation was to supply men to work for him on the island, which it had.[12] After six months' discussion no decision had been reached, and Bell and the company agreed to refer the case to an arbitrator. Even with arbitra-tion no agreement could be made. Settlement was made more difficult when the company disbanded and reformed in 1637, and only its individual members could be sued. Bell took the members of the company to court in 1638.[13]

Details of the litigation are scanty, but St. John handled the case for the members. In November 1638, the lord keeper upheld the company, ruling that particular members of the company were not liable for agreements made under the common seal of the company, which, presumably, was the defense outlined by St. John. Philip Bell, however, was not mollified by the decision and continued to demand that the company pay him some compensation. The dispute was not settled until July 1640, when Bell accepted £50 in full payment of his claims.[14]

The body that has come to be known as the Short Parliament was also summoned in 1640 in response to Charles's need for money to continue the war with Scotland. The Short Parliament marks the beginning of St. John's political career, as he was chosen to stand for Totnes, Devon. In recent years historians have perhaps too readily assumed that the Short Parliament was an obstinate and intractable body. It is true that Charles's policies had generated unrest and hostility, with the issues of religious discontent and arbitrary taxation predominating. Nevertheless, there was no determined onslaught on the policies of the "Personal Rule." Clarendon thought that the Short Parliament was a potentially manageable body, and St. John considered it to be decidedly timid.[15] It is certainly possible that if the king's advisers had seized the initiative with a proposal asking for parliamentary consent for Ship Money and offered concessions on religion, they might have secured a substantial grant of money. In his Ship Money speech in 1637, St. John had given every indication that there was nothing wrong with Ship Money except for the fact that it had not been approved by Parliament.

St. John's role in the early stages of these proceedings is fairly clear. He was not a dominating figure, but his wide constitutional learning commanded respect. In a speech on 17 April, Pym divided the basic grievances of the Commons into four categories: parliamentary liberties, religion, affairs of State, and matters of property.[16] Religious grievances included the perceived encouragement by the Crown of the Romish religion, the introduction of Romish ceremonies, and the printing of popish books. On these matters St. John was fairly quiet. But when a Mr. Herbert stated that questioning the King's right to dissolve Parliament amounted to "trenching upon his prerogative,"[17] St. John rose quickly to dispute him, denying that questioning the dissolution in any way touched the royal prerogative. What happened in 1629, said St. John, was a matter of fact, and, as a matter of right, the king had called Parliament by the Great Seal of England and not by his bare command. Therefore, it could not be dissolved by his word alone, and the dissolution of 1629 was illegal.[18]

On 22 April, St. John made his first recorded comments about religion, concurring with a claim by Pym that acts passed by a convocation could not bind the laity or make canons universal. This proposition was designed to prevent religious innovations from being imposed, as they had been in the 1630s, by Laud and a gathering of bishops. No canons should be binding, argued Pym and St. John, unless approved by Parliament.[19]

Although of lesser urgency when compared to Laud or Scotland as a parliamentary grievance, Ship Money was still a burning issue in 1640. Thus, when the lord keeper made a speech defending the integrity of the King and the King's right to Ship Money, and imploring the Commons to first vote supply before discussing grievances, St. John was quick to respond, although he was not the only member of Commons to oppose it. Pym, Sir Walter Earle, John Glynn, and Robert Holborne all criticized the Lord Keeper's speech.[20] St. John did more than merely speak aganst Ship Money. On 4 May 1640 he moved that the legality of Ship Money be put to the question.[21] Not surprisingly, this proposal produced an uproar. In effect, St. John was proposing that the Commons overturn a decision already rendered by the courts.

St. John may have pressed the issue of Ship Money too far. Even some of his friends appear to have been annoyed by his insistence on the critical importance of Ship Money. Later the same day, John Hampden said that he thought there were other issues besides Ship Money that warranted the Commons's attention. In Hampden's opinion, the great burdens imposed on the counties in religious affairs were a far greater cause for alarm. St. John, however, was not daunted. He replied again that Ship Money was basic to everything. It was necessary to make provision against all similar exactions (for example, religious innovations imposed without parliamentary consent), or else there might be another unfortunate judgment in a new matter. St. John reminded the Commons that when Edward III was threatened in the fourteenth century with the French coming by sea and the Scots coming by land, he still went to Parliament for the money he used to resist them. Later, on 4 May, St. John suggested that the Commons grant twelve subsidies in return for the abolition of Ship Money.[22]

The vote on the legality of Ship Money, of course, was never taken, because, on the next day, 5 May 1640, Charles dissolved Parliament. Rumors had reached him that the Commons intended to present him with a petition against carrying on his war with the Convenanters.[23] The existence of such rumors should not have surprised him. The speeches of several MPs suggested that Parliament might pursue this course of action. In addition, just before the dissolution, another member, Harbottle Grimston, argued that the invasions on the liberties of citizens were in more urgent need of rebuttal than Scottish incursions over the northern border.[24] Exasperated, the king feared that his opponents had reached an agreement with the Scots. The most obvious way to thwart them was to dissolve Parliament. At its dissolution Parliament had been sitting barely three weeks.

Reaction to the dissolution was mixed. Many members were embittered. Clarendon wrote of a "great damp" seizing men's spirits at the time of dismissal.[25] But one man was not bothered in the least. Within an hour after the dissolution, Clarendon encountered St. John in a corridor, and, in a famous passage, described St. John's reaction:

> Within an hour after the dissolving, Mr. Hyde met Mr. St. John, who had naturally a great cloud in his face and very seldom was known to smile, but then had a most cheerful aspect, and seeing the other [Hyde] melancholic as in truth he was from his heart, asked him, "What troubled him?", who answered, "That same thing which troubled him, he believed that troubled most good men; that in such a time of confusion so wise a Parliament, which alone could only have found remedy for it, was so unreasonably dismissed." The other [St. John] answered with a little warmth, "That all was well: and that it must be worse before it could be better; and that this Parliament would never have done what was necessary to be done, as indeed it would not what he and his friends thought was necessary.[26]

This passage indicated that St. John felt a considerable amount of alienation not only against the Crown but against moderates as well. What he thought should be done is clear from his speeches: overturn the Ship Money decision and compel the Crown to obtain parliamentary consent for any additional taxation. If Clarendon's retrospective account is correct and St. John feared that sterner measures would be necessary to restrain the monarchy, it cannot have bolstered his waning confidence in the Crown to find that his Ship Money papers were seized at the end of the session and that a number of parliamentary leaders—including the earls of Warwick, Lord Saye and Sele, Hampden, and Pym—were briefly arrested.[27]

In the summer following the dissolution of the Short Parliament, Strafford labored furiously to revive the English Army. But resistance to his efforts within the counties and within the government doomed them to failure. Public enthusiasm for war, already low, was further eroded by a series of blunders by Laud. Laud not only decided to keep the Convocation in session after the dissolution of Parliament—in defiance of long-established tradition—but also guided the passage of a new series of canons, which, under the circumstances, were incredibly ill-timed. One of the canons instructed the clergy to preach the doctrine of the divine right of kings in the most uncompromising terms, and another pledged the clergy to accept the government of the Church as then established. The Convocation also granted the King six clerical subsidies, worth approximately £20,000 each, amounting to a £120,000 benevolence from the clergy.

In the summer of 1640 the Scots again invaded England. By 29 August they had captured Newcastle. With the English Army battered and mutinous, Charles clutched at a last hope and summoned a Great Council of Peers to York to ask for their advice. But he opened the assembly by announcing his intention to call Parliament and making clear his continuing hostility toward the Scots. Charles had, however, no immediate choice but to settle with the Scots, and an agreement was quickly reached at Ripon, requiring the crown to pay the Scottish Army £850 a day until the final peace was complete. This agreement, in effect, shackled Charles to Parliament and forced him to summon it in order to pay off the Scots. The body that came to be known as the Long Parliament convened on 3 November 1640.

The men who assembled at Westminster in the fall of 1640 were deeply conservative men who had not the slightest thought of armed rebellion or of dismantling the monarchy. Some, however, did have private grievances with the Crown. Of the original 547 members, nearly 60 had resisted royal demands for loans; 18 had been imprisoned for their refusal to pay; an additional 20 had been imprisoned for other expressions of dissatisfaction; and 50 had in some way opposed Ship Money.[28] Often discordant and contentious, these men were loosely united behind a vague political vision consisting of dreams of a Reformed Church and a Godly Commonwealth, local particularism, and the restoration of an imagined Ancient Constitution. No specific plan for reform existed, but most members believed that the first step in the reform process included the removal of the King's errant ministers and their replacement with men who inspired Parliament's trust.

Guiding this undertaking required the skills of several men, although no particular person could be said to be in control.[29] Foremost among those who aspired to leadership was John Pym of Tavistock in Devonshire. A short, pudgy man, Pym had served in Parliaments since 1614, his seat, like St. John's in 1640, having been obtained through the generosity of the earl of Bedford. Pym's career in the 1620s was undistinguished, but in the 1640s he had emerged as a dogged and formidable adversary of certain aspects of royal policy. A convinced Puritan, he believed that England was gripped by the terrifying specter of a Catholic conspiracy to subvert true religion and English liberties. At the same time, he was instinctively conservative, opposed to new and unfamiliar ideas and ways of thinking, and determined to preserve as much as possible of existing institutions.[30]

Closely connected to Pym was John Hampden of Buckinghamshire, a member of Parliament since the 1620s. Hampden, of course, had been thrust into prominence through his refusal to pay Ship Money. Unlike Pym, Hampden was a man of vast wealth, and he was also widely admired for his gentleness, courtly manners, and integrity. But at least one person expressed some doubts about Hampden's character. Clarendon believed that Hampden's unpretentious and accommodating ways merely cloaked his determination to wrest authority from the Crown. "After he observed how the house was like to be inclined, he took up the argument . . . and craftily so stated in that he commonly conducted it to the conclusion he desired; and if he found he could not do that, he was never without the dexterity to avert it to another time and to prevent determining anything negative which might prove inconvenient in the future."[31]

Leadership also came from the House of Lords, and in particular from Francis Russell, the fourth earl of Bedford, who had already exerted a discernible influence on Parliament by procuring seats. A man of immense wealth, Bedford enjoyed an income of £15,000 a year, derived mainly from monastic lands acquired by the first earl after the dissolution of the monasteries. Bedford supported the Petition of Right in 1628 and favored the redress of grievances before voting supply in 1640. Since 1614 he had secured the return of John Pym from Tavistock, and since 1629 he had employed Oliver St. John to manage his legal affairs. Like Pym, Bedford was a conservative with no interest in the comprehensive change in the state of society. He was too wealthy for that, thought Clarendon.[32] Although a Puritan and author of ten folio volumes of religious meditations, he found no difficulty in dining with Puritans one night and Laud the next.[33] Moderate, conservative, but profoundly disturbed by the events of the past two decades, Bedford was willing to support a reasonable program of reform for existing institutions, but he had no wish to disturb them.

Compared with these men, St. John must be regarded as a lesser, but not secondary, figure, who appeared to grow in importance during this period. At the time of the Short Parliament, Clarendon thought St. John to be "much governed" by Pym. By the time of the Long Parliament, Clarendon said that St. John was "in firm and entire conjunction with the other two [Pym and Hampden]."[34] St. John's carriage and demeanor also left a firm imprint on Clarendon. A writer whose ability to sum up character appears to be unrivaled among Civil War memoirists, Clarendon described St. John as a "man reserved, and of a dark and clouded countenance, very proud, conversing with very few, and those, men of his own humor and inclinations."[35] Clarendon also believed that Pym, Hampden, Bedford, St. John, and, later, Sir Henry Vane the Younger were all of a "most intimate and entire trust" and were "the engine which moved all the rest."[36]

When the Long Parliament finally met, its first move was to impeach Strafford and Laud for treason. Pym naturally was the prime mover in these proceedings. At this stage St. John made only some brief comments, but, giving a hint of his future feelings, he said that the Commons should pursue Laud and Strafford even if the Lords refused.[37]

St. John's legal expertise was instantly and eagerly sought when the Commons began debating the legality of Ship Money. On 27 November 1640, Sir Walter Earle asked St. John to explain what was at stake in the Ship Money question. St. John replied that the opinions of the judges were now the grievances and not Ship Money itself. But he apparently did not mean it. Almost in the next breath, he said, "Ship Money overthrows the Magna Carta and all our liberties. If Ship Money stands, Parliaments have no power."[38]

A committee of which St. John was a member was then formed to give an opinion on Ship Money. On 7 December, St. John reported for the committee, stating the committee's opinion that the King could not, under any pretense of danger or necessity, levy a tax without parliamentary consent. The Commons then dispatched St. John to inform the Lords of their decision.[39]

Hot words passed the next day between St. John and Sir John Finch over Ship Money. St. John accused Finch of misrepresenting the opinion of one of the judges, Denham, to the King over Ship Money. After the first issue of writs in 1635, Denham had received a letter from Finch soliciting his opinion. When Denham became too ill to present it to the king in person, Finch delivered it and reported on its contents. Denham later discovered that Finch's rendition was less than accurate and incorrectly favored Finch's own view.[40]

At a conference of both houses the subject shifted to religion, as Parliament debated whether the acts of synods could bind the subjects of England. The arguments for imposition by convocation were presented, interestingly enough, by Robert Holborne, St. John's associate at Lincoln's Inn and his partner in the Hampden case. Holborne argued that canons not directly against the law and confirmed by the Crown should be considered binding. Canons pronounced in the past under numerous monarchs, from Henry VIII to James I, frequently had been instituted without parliamentary approval. Moreover, concluded Holborne, surely the Church should be governed by itself and not be subject to the whims of impressionable laymen.[41]

St. John spoke for those opposed to the canons, attacking imposition by convocation on constitutional grounds, by arguing that laws affecting the entire country must be approved by Parliament. Matters of religion, said he, had always been determined by Parliament. Consent of the Reformation Parliament had been necessary before Henry VIII rebuilt the English Church, and Elizabeth had obtained parliamentary approval for her religious settlement.[42] Others opposed the canons on theological grounds. John Maynard asserted that the arguments of the clergy in this case were the same as those by which the pope claimed his false and odious power. The clergy were simply too ambitious. When the matter came to a vote, the Commons resolved against the right of the clergy to make canons.[43]

On 19 December, St. John's antipathy toward Sir John Finch, the Lord Keeper, surfaced again, evidenced by St. John's introduction of articles of impeachment against him. St. John's action reflected both personal animosity and constitutional outrage. St. John believed that Finch had deliberately sabotaged the judges' decision in the Ship Money case. Moreover, to St. John and others, Finch was a symbol of the evils of the Court. As judge and Lord Keeper, Finch was inextricably bound to the policies of the 1630s to which many members objected. The principal items of indictment against him, as enumerated by St. John, included his attempt to prevent Sir John Eliot's speech at the close of the Parliament of 1629, "malpractices on the Bench in 1635 for the purpose of extending the royal forest of Essex beyond its legal boundaries," and his conduct in the Hampden case.[44] St. John suggested further that Finch be allowed to defend himself, which he did in a long and elaborate speech on 21 December 1640. But before the articles against him could be finalized, Finch fled to Holland, arriving at the Hague on 31 December 1640.[45]

Finch's flight did not deter St. John from inveighing against both Finch and Ship Money. No doubt, in St. John's mind there was very little difference between the two. In a speech on 14 January 1641, to a joint conference of the Lords and the Commons, he expressed some fresh ideas on the matter. The purpose of the conference, said St. John, was to advise the Lords on how far the Commons had proceeded in the Ship Money matter, which St. John described as "a means by which the property of our goods and the liberty of our persons were not only taken away, but our very lives endangered." Moreover, the judges, who should have been vigilant and stern against such blatant trespasses of the rights of Englishmen, became, said St. John, "through the brocage and solicitation of the Lord Finch, late keeper of the Great Seal of England, the destroyers and subverters of the same."[46]

St. John then delivered another highly charged attack on Ship Money. His complaint was not, he said, that Ship Money was levied; it was the right by which it was claimed. If the recent manner of levying Ship Money was legal, said St. John, "our birthright, our ancestral right, our condition of continuing as free subjects is lost; that of late there has been endeavor to reduce us to the state of villeinage, nay, to a lower."[47] St. John also included a number of remarks apparently intended to reassure his audience of his respect for the Crown, declaring that none of these violations reflected any discredit on the King. His majesty's justice, after all, he said, was "the fairest diamond of the crown."[48] Responsibility for the uproar over Ship Money must be placed with the judges and with Finch in particular.[49] St. John's speech was apparently quite effective. On 20 January 1641 the Lords passed a series of resolutions condemning Ship Money.

Perhaps the most puzzling episode of St. John's career concerns his appointment as the King's Solicitor in January 1641. Unfortunately, little can be added here to existing knowledge. According to Clarendon, St. John's appointment was part of an enterprise, conceived by the earl of Bedford, to appoint St. John and several others—including Bedford himself, Pym, and Lord Saye—to high office in return for securing a reasonable financial settlement for the king. Bedford hoped to solve the problem of evil counselors by persuading Charles to appoint those who inspired Parliament's trust.[50]

Several contemporaries believed that Bedford's plan might succeed. As Sir John Temple remarked, "I understand the King is brought into dislike of those counsels that he hath formerly followed, and therefore resolves to steer another course." Temple then reported the rumored appointments of Bedford, Pym, and Saye. In early February 1641, Charles named Bedford, Hertford, Essex, Bristol, Saye, Saville, Hamilton, and Mandeville to the Privy Council, thus displaying a modest interest in reform, or at least his willingness to take a shot at buying off his critics.[51]

Bedford's scheme, of course, failed. Evidence remains scanty, but as far as anyone can determine, it failed because no compromise could be reached over Strafford. Charles apparently believed that, in return for his concessions on appointments, Strafford must be spared. But Strafford aroused such hostility that sparing him appeared to be impossible. Robert Baillie described the dilemma of the marquis of Hamilton: "If he denied to deal for Strafford, he should offend the

King. If he assayed to deal further for him he should lose Parliament and us all."[52] By the end of February it was clear that schemes based on bridge appointments would not succeed. Charles would not sacrifice Strafford, and the Commons would not agree to spare him. This stalemate continued until 9 March, when Bedford, Saye, Essex, Mandeville, and Brook, to the dismay of Bristol and Saville, supported the Commons in their pursuit of Strafford. Bedford's scheme thus collapsed, but St. John nonetheless landed on his feet as solicitor.

The ideas St. John expressed on Ship Money in January 1641 represented a considerable advance over those he held in 1637. In 1637 he had questioned primarily the king's failure to observe proper legal channels. In 1641 he challenged the right by which Ship Money was levied and the judges' upholding of that right. When the judges had upheld the right by which Ship Money was levied, St. John claimed, all the ancestral rights that allowed Englishmen to exist as free subjects had been threatened. St. John then expounded on a new definition of treason by which the judges could be implicated. The judges' votes in the Ship Money case, he asserted, were in substance contrary to the laws of the realm, the rights of property, and the liberties of subjects, and contrary to former resolutions passed in Parliament, such as the Petition of Right. Ship Money was a tax imposed without parliamentary consent, and the Petition had been passed to prevent such exactions. The judges, who were under oath to uphold the law and who were entrusted by the king to render accurate interpretations of the law, had knowingly violated their oaths of office and the trust conferred on them.[53]

Although fortified by precedent, many of St. John's arguments clearly went beyond the law. At various times between 1640 and 1641, St. John had argued that Parliament should overturn a decision already rendered by the courts, that Parliament possessed the power to prevent its own dissolution, that treason could be committed against Parliament as well as against the King, and that Parliament had the right in certain instances to supersede the common law and inferior courts. The man who attacked the King for ignoring the law in the Ship Money case now appeared to be willing to tamper with it himself. In the past few years important work by Caroline Hibbard and Anthony Fletcher has demonstrated that many in England were driven down the path to resistance by fears of an insidious and pervasive Catholic conspiracy.[54] St. John's relentless pursuit of Finch and his repeated return to *Rex* v. *Hampden* suggests that he perceived an utterly different conspiracy. Like many of his contemporaries, St. John believed that law was immemorial. In his view statutes declared what the law was; they did not create it. The law itself was sovereign, and the judges alone could divine its mysteries. However, by the 1630s, both the prerogative courts and the common law courts that had upheld Ship Money were perceived by many as merely the instruments of royal tyranny. During Charles's Personal Rule the courts had enforced monopolies and ridden unchallenged over the property rights. Charles himself had displayed a particular arrogance. In 1626 he had dismissed Chief Justice Crew for refusing to admit the legality of the forced loan, and by 1637 he had apparently reduced the judges to a state where they were unable to restrict Laudian innovation or resist the apparent attempts to circumvent due process by men like Finch.

With the judiciary intimidated, St. John concluded that Parliament was the only organ of government that could be trusted. As long as the wisdom of the judges could be thwarted, none of England's problems could be solved. If the court's powers were returned to their proper station, the subversion of law and religion could be corrected. St. John had thus arrived at a crude conception of parliamentary sovereignty, apparently designed as a temporary expedient until the courts could regain their authority.

It is also clear that St. John was not always in positive agreement with the men opposing aspects of royal policy. Historians have generally accepted Clarendon's assessment of St. John as a man acting in "firm and entire conjunction" with Pym, Hampden, and Holles. Yet, St. John often appears as an anomaly. The others do not seem to have regarded Ship Money with the same sense of urgency. St. John's differences on this score with Hampden have already been noticed, made all the more striking because Hampden had retained St. John in the first place. Important differerences also existed between St. John and Pym. On the one hand Pym believed that England was gripped by a massive Catholic conspiracy. On the other St. John stressed the enormity of the legal conspiracy and seemingly regarded it as far more serious and sinister than the Catholic plot. St. John never expressed himself publicly on the finer points of Church doctrine and structure, although he seems to have embraced clear anti-episcopal, Erastian beliefs, framed around a perceptible, but cloudy, Puritanism.[55] At a time when it would have been easy and natural for him to do so, St. John never connected the legal and papist conspiracies. He never blamed the subversion of the judiciary on Catholic designs and made no allusions to them in his major speeches. At one point he even argued that "papists might be servants in ordinary court if they were licensed."[56] His other writings offer little assistance in elucidating his religious beliefs. A theological commonplace book in his possession, apparently compiled by members of his family, demonstrates a familiarity with the basic tenets of Elizabethan and early Stuart Puritanism and with the moral outlook of Cicero and Roman philosophy. St. John also composed a lengthy commentary on the Epistle to the Ephesians. But few concrete religious convictions, excepting his Erastianism and his hostility toward the bishops, emerge from any of his writings.[57]

Moreover, whereas St. John regarded Finch as the principal instrument of the legal conspiracy, Pym—according to Clarendon and Sir Edward Nicholas—made several efforts to prevent the proceedings against Finch.[58] Given his loathing for Finch, St. John's fierce opposition to episcopacy must have made Pym uneasy. Pym and St. John clashed on other issues as well. On 27 November, Pym moved to obtain a grant of tonnage and poundage, only to be challenged by St. John and Sir Walter Earle.[59] Clarendon listed St. John as one of the authors of the Root and Branch Bill, and, elsewhere, St. John claimed to deplore the bishops because they had plotted treason since the time of St. Augustine and were decidedly anti-monarchical.[60] By contrast, Pym, described by Clarendon as "not of those furious resolutions against the Church as the other leading men were," withheld his support for Root and Branch until June 1641. Even in support of the bill, Pym sounded a conciliatory note, explaining that provisions would be made for the deposed ministers and that additional safeguards could be inserted into the bill.[61]

Differences between St. John and Pym also surfaced over the attainder of Thomas Wentworth, the earl of Strafford. Like many in the Commons, Pym perceived Strafford as the architect of the Catholic conspiracy—in Macaulay's famous, but melodramatic, words, "the lost archangel, the dark satan of apostasy." The Commons' case against Strafford was based on the treason statute of 1352, which defined treason as compassing or imagining the death of the King or the Queen or levying war against the King or the Queen. The committee charged with drawing up the indictment assembled nine general and twenty-eight particular charges. The critical charges were contained in the particular articles fifteen and twenty-three. In article fifteen Strafford was accused of issuing a warrant for the billeting of soldiers on Irish householders. In article twenty-three he was charged with advising Charles I that Charles was "loose and absolved from all rules of government" and that Charles might use an Irish Army to reduce England to obedience.[62] At the core of the indictment was the idea that, although treason in the specific charges could not always be proved conclusively, Strafford's accumulation of misdeeds amounted to an endeavor to subvert law and divide the king and his people. Accumulative treason and subversion of law were not covered by the statute of 1352. This weakness, however, did not deter Strafford's inquisitors. As Pym expressed it, Strafford's treason went "beyond words."[63]

The trial opened in Westminster Hall on 22 March 1641. Almost immediately, the Commons' case at law and fact began to sputter as Strafford mustered a combative and resourceful defense. Ignoring the broader aspects of his indictment and refusing to be drawn into any general statement, Strafford disputed tenaciously the factual accuracy of the charges against him and repeatedly cast serious doubts on the competence and reliability of the witnesses against him. He also derided the Commons' theory of "accumulative" treason, asking if "a thousand misdeameanors will not make one felony, shall twenty-eight misdemeanors heighten it to treason?" As well, Strafford skillfully exploited a critical weakness in the Commons' case regarding article twenty-three. Pym insisted that Strafford's alleged advice to Charles that an army in Ireland could be used to reduce subjects in "this kingdom" constituted treason by statute. But it was not clear by the phrase "this kingdom" whether Strafford intended Scotland or England. Moreover, by the statute of 1 Edw. VI c. 12, two witnesses were required in treason cases. Pym could produce only one, the elder Vane, whose testimony was contradicted by several other witnesses.[64]

Thus, Strafford had exposed several serious weaknesses in the Commons' case, both in fact and law, and by early April it was clear that Strafford was gaining sympathy and support. Robert Baillie reported that Strafford was gaining converts daily "among the more simple sort."[65] With the case against Strafford in disarray, the Commons began to consider abandoning impeachment and resorting to a bill of attainder. Impeachment proceedings required that Strafford be convicted by charges that could be sustained by law and proved to the satisfaction of the House of Lords. Attainder, on the other hand, was simply an act of Parliament declaring that Strafford's death was necessary to the safety of the State. Attainder could be passed without formal proofs of Strafford's guilt as long as the majority believed that the presumption of guilt was strong enough. Thus, attainder provided the perfect solution for those members who were convinced of Strafford's treason, but were troubled by the difficulty of proving it and did not wish to have the law distorted too severely to secure the conviction.

On 10 April, Sir Arthur Haselrig introduced into the House of Commons a Bill of Attainder against Strafford. The decision to implement attainder, however, was not unanimous. John Pym was initially its most formidable opponent. Reluctant to offend the Lords and determined to preserve the harmony between the Houses, Pym—

along with Hampden, Strode, and Earle—favored a continuation of the trial. Summoning his full powers of persuasion and political dexterity, Pym convinced the house to postpone the bill's second reading.[66]

Postponement, however, did not yield any advantage for Pym. Oliver St. John took up the cause of attainder vigorously, while at the same time the case against Strafford in terms of impeachment continued to erode. D'Ewes and others detected a growing shift toward Strafford by mid-April.[67] On 13 April, Strafford delivered a moving summary of his defense. Between 14 and 17 April, Robert Holborne, Sir John Culpepper, and Strafford's counsel Richard Lane advanced further arguments on the earl's behalf.[68] In regard to Strafford's alleged subversion of fundamental laws, Edmund Waller demanded that these fundamental laws be defined before Strafford could be accused of breaking them. Waller was shouted down, but the consternation he provoked was enough to convince Strafford that deliverance was at hand, and he returned to the Tower singing hymns of thanksgiving.[69]

Faced with serious problems in proving his case at law and in fact, Pym finally recognized that attainder was the most practical alternative. On the Monday following Lane's speech, Pym at last joined St. John in a determined attempt to seal Strafford's fate by attainder.[70] On 21 April, by a margin of 204–59, the Commons approved the attainder.

The next problem was to justify attainder to the Lords, and St. John undertook this task on 29 April 1641 in his famous speech to the Lords. He began by assuring the Lords that attainder was not a last resort or a desperate measure. Rather, it was the proper procedure for deciding doubtful cases and he contended that in all former ages Parliament had been consulted if doubts of law arose. Parliamentary scrutiny served to remove doubts and would allow members to arrive at a decision based on "the private satisfaction of each man's conscience."[71] St. John also challenged Strafford's claim that 1 Henry IV had regarding treason that 25 Edw III had conferred upon Parliament. The act of 1 Henry IV, St. John claimed, had been invoked only to reverse the illegal acts of Richard II, not to repeal the declaratory power of Parliament. Moreover, subsequent legislation under both Edward VI and Mary restored the definition of treason propounded by 25 Edw III and conferred on Parliament the right to decide doubtful cases.[72]

For most of the remainder of his speech St. John wrestled with the thornier problems of the Commons's case. Like the trial managers, St. John could demonstrate with relative ease that levying war against the

King was treason. What was more difficult was proving that Strafford's actions amounted to the levying of war. St. John's reliance on attainder enabled him to claim that Strafford's advice to Charles—that he was "loose and absolved from the rules of government" and that he could use an army to Ireland to "reduce this kingdom"—constituted treason even though there was only one witness.[73] But Strafford and Lane repeatedly questioned how the use of a handful of soldiers in Ireland amounted to treason, and certainly Strafford had never advised anyone to oppose the King.

St. John responded to this defense in two ways. First, he reiterated the Commons's earlier arguments of accumulative treason and that the overthrow of any statute constituted a war against the king, adding that Strafford had "assumed an arbitrary power over the lives, liberties, and estates of his majesties' subjects." St. John then introduced his own subtle refinement by advancing the doctrine of constructively compassing the King's death. By this doctrine St. John meant that Strafford—through his arbitrary actions and by his advice to the king to exercise arbitrary power—was attempting to make the king so odious that his people would rise against him. Strafford was thus guilty of endangering the king's life in a possible rebellion, and this advice certainly entailed compassing his death. The earl's advice to Charles about the exercise of arbitrary authority, said St. John, amounted to the same thing as offering the King a "poisoned drink while telling him it is a cordial." It would not matter that the poison was repelled; the malicious intent of the giver would still be clear.[74] In this way St. John could argue that Strafford's actions still constituted treason even though there clearly was no opposition to the king involved.

St. John then dwelled at some length on the question of parliamentary jurisdiction in Ireland. The Irish statute of 18 Henry VI c.3 made it treason to impose "hoblers, kearns, English rebels, and Irish enemies" on subjects in Ireland. Strafford's issuance of a warrant to Robert Savile for billeting soldiers on Irish subjects, according to Pym, was a violation of that statute. During the trial Strafford countered this argument by asserting that he could not be tried in England on an Irish statute. St. John replied that, as Parliament could make laws for Ireland and laws made in England applied to Ireland *in omnibus,* Parliament could certainly exercise its power through a bill of attainder. "If Strafford is not triable here," said St. John, "he is triable nowhere."[75]

At the conclusion of his speech, St. John returned to the issue of Parliament's legislative power to attain Strafford. St. John first defended the concept of subversion of law as a common law treason. If

Strafford's actions were not treason, he said, "England's but a piece of earth wherein so many men have their commorancy and abode, without ranks or distinction among men, without property in anything further than possessions, no law to punish the murdering or robbing of one another." The idea of treason by subversion of law, St. John continued, provides security for the subject, and however ancient it might be, "like gold, it has lost little or nothing of its value."[76] Despite the many alterations of treason law since 1352, he reminded members that Parliament still retained one crucial right, specified in 25 Edw III. That statute provided that, in cases not directly covered under it, the "judges shall not proceed until the case be judged in Parliament, whether it be treason or not."[77]

To members still not convinced, St. John offered in almost shotgun fashion a barrage of other justifications as to why Stafford should be made as "miserable" as the law could make a man. Responding to the objection that the resort to attainder amounted to an ex post facto indictment, St. John replied that, since Strafford had denied law to others, "why should he have any himself; why should not that be done to him that himself would have done to others." St. John then added his outrageous suggestion that

> It's true, we give law to hares and deers, because they be beasts of chase; it was never accounted either cruelty or foul play to knock foxes and wolves on the head as they can be found; because these be beasts of prey: The Warrener sets traps for powlcats and other vermin, for preservation of the warren.[78]

Moreover, said St. John, Strafford was well aware that he had "offended the law" and that he should be prepared to suffer the consequences. "Errors in great things, as war and marriage," St. John suggested—perhaps to inject some humor into a three-hour speech—"they allow no time for repentance." More importantly, in his conclusion St. John also elaborated on his conception of parliamentary rights. Parliament, he insisted, had the power to convict Strafford, if all other arguments failed, because Parliament is

> both the physician and the patient. If the body be distempered, it hath the power to open a vein, to let out the corrupt blood for curing itself; if one member be poisoned or gangr[en]ed, it hath the power to cut it off for the preservation of the rest.[79]

The concept of Parliament as both physician and patient, developed by St. John in the Strafford speech, was the logical extension of his Ship Money doctrines. By his various attempts to recast and broaden the scope of parliamentary power, St. John moved beyond the trite and naive notion that Parliament was merely protecting the King from the perfidious associates who had beguiled him and that removal of these errant ministers would restore the damaged Constitution. St. John perceived the need for Parliament not only to restore its rights but to extend them. At various times between 1640 and 1642, he conferred on Parliament the right to challenge the king's power of dissolution, the right to overturn decisions already rendered by the courts, the right to determine the nation's religious settlement, and now the right to remove "poisoned and gangr[en]ed" members of which it did not approve. He attempted to extend Parliament's authority by claiming that treason could be committed against it as well as the King. Clearly, St. John's ideas emerged not from detached, theoretical reflection about the distribution of authority, but from specific objections to the exercise of that authority. Like most of his contemporaries, St. John believed that government was founded on monarchy as the head and protector of the body politic, and that government operated through the interplay of the Crown, the Houses of Parliament, and the courts. Parliament as an institution was not sovereign and was by no means equal to the king, but it did possess the right to offer counsel and was the only channel through which the king could legislate. Time, custom, history, and experience demonstrated that this system was the best that could be devised. The English did not fear bad kings; they feared only an alteration of the system. But because the exact dividing line between the rights of the monarchy and those of Parliament was vague and imprecise, and the relative strengths of king and Parliament might shift depending on the temperament of the king or the composition of Parliament, the courts were expected to provide a stern and unchanging bulwark to protect the rights of both institutions, to resolve disputes, and to maintain the security of living under rule of law. Maintenance of legal channels was imperative because most observers believed that their lives, liberties, and property were protected by law and that these could not be touched, seized, or diminished simply by royal decree.

But the system did not provide any remedy for a King who, by appointing obsequious judges and dismissing or intimidating independent ones, attempted to secure a judiciary amenable to his will. The King was supposed to take counsel, but no one was prepared to say to what extent he was compelled to follow its advice. By 1641, Charles I had displayed little inclination to consider, much less take, the advice of his representative body. With the evidence provided by the Ship Money case and during Strafford's trial, it was possible for many observers to believe that an alteration of government was not only in progress, it had already occurred, that the courts could not prevent it, and that the common law and property were being destroyed. When the King himself abused or failed to prevent the abuse of the machinery of government by others in order to elevate his prerogative rights over the rule of law, Parliament became the only recourse for those determined to restore rule of law. For such members as St. John, Parliament must necesssarily extend its traditional responsibilities, even if this extension meant further alteration of government and law. As St. John remarked about Strafford, "He who would deny the law to others, why should he have any himself?" Like so many of his contemporaries, St. John was pinned between the Scylla of obedience and the Charybdis of continuing alteration.

3

Rendering to Caesar and Parliament

It is likely now that the earl of Strafford is dispatched that business will go faster. . . . What course will be taken in it I cannot judge; but I doubt not, if they make a change, such things will be contained in it as cannot be foreseen; and I fear if somebody be not there present to make a defense or disprove them, they may be taken *pro confesso,* which may be a ruin to us all.[1]

Thomas Wentworth, the earl of Strafford, was executed on 12 May 1641, and with these words a parliamentary observer named Robert Reade assessed legislative prospects in May 1641. Reade correctly predicted that Strafford's death would alter significantly the course and temper of Parliament and that unforeseen directions would be taken. He was, however, a little vague about the precise nature of these changes. Retrospectively, it is possible to discern two important re-orientations in the politics of the Long Parliament in May 1641. The first came in the immediate aftermath of the trial of the earl of Strafford; the second came in the aftermath of his execution. St. John played a minor role in the first, but he was critically important to the second. Most studies of the Long Parliament, rightly more concerned with other matters and the larger pattern of parliamentary politics, have examined this period, but they may not have yet appreciated all its meanings.[2]

Strafford's trial and its aftermath, however, altered decisively the character of politics in the Long Parliament. Fears that Charles would reprieve Strafford, as he had tried to reprieve Father John Goodman in January, surfaced immediately. Essex, after all, followed up his celebrated "stone dead hath no fellow" pronouncement by explaining his concern that Charles, once Parliament disbanded, would grant Strafford a pardon and bring him back into the government.[3] Charles did nothing to dispel these fears. He permitted Sir John Suckling to raise soldiers in London and attempted to reinforce the garrison in the Tower with a hundred men under the command of an officer of his own choosing. He also made two imprudent, even reckless, speeches.

On 28 April he informed both houses that he would not dismiss the English Catholics at court nor would he disband the Irish Army until Parliament had voted the subsidy. On 1 May he informed the Lords that he was convinced of Strafford's innocence and would under no circumstance agree to pass the bill against his life, clearly implying that his royal rejection of the case against Strafford was sufficient reason for the Lords to reject it. It is difficult to gauge the impact of Charles's speech, but several foreign correspondents believed that Charles was preparing a counter stroke, and they predicted civil war.[4]

Politics then shifted into a new key. Removal of errant ministers remained a critical focus for most members, but fears of Charles's potential for revenge and duplicity, previously submerged, now had to be considered. Members were aware of Charles's personal devotion to Strafford, and of his pledge, even after the passage of the attainder bill in the Commons, to save him.[5] Responding to fears that Charles might move to save Strafford, Pym implemented some dramatic measures to forestall royal intervention. First, Pym proposed that members sign a loyalty oath, the Protestation of 3 May, warning that a design to subvert fundamental law by the introduction of arbitrary and tyrannical government in England through wicked counsels still existed. At the same time the Commons passed a bill to make it illegal to adjourn, prorogue, or dissolve Parliament without its own consent. Pym rallied the unconverted by revealing the existence of a plot to bring the English Army south to intimidate Parliament into sparing Strafford.[6] It has been suggested that the measure for the continuance of Parliament was not a challenge to royal authority, even though it took away a right reserved traditionally for the King. In fact, some believe, it was a measure designed simply to keep Parliament from disbanding before adequate revenues for the King could be secured.[7] But the logic here is strained. Charles did not need new legislation to keep Parliament in session. He already possessed that power himself. It seems plausible, in the highly charged atmosphere of early May, to regard the continuance act as a means to protect Parliament from the possibility—expressed, as we have seen, by the earl of Essex—that Charles would dissolve Parliament and then pardon Strafford.

By marshaling fears of royal counterstroke, Pym had persuaded Parliament to take, albeit reluctantly, some revolutionary steps. The members who signed the Protestation of 3 May continued to deplore the designs against their liberties by papists and evil counselors. But they also proclaimed themselves to be the true defenders of the Church of England, the rights of Parliament, and His Majesty's royal person. The shift toward Parliament as the protector of the body politic was a significant step. It was also noted by St. John in his

speech justifying Strafford's attainder to the Lords. St. John declared
that "Parliament is the great body politic; it comprehends all from the
king to the beggar."[8] While there were medieval precedents for the
bill to prevent the king from dissolving Parliament without its consent
and the Triennial Act, both were clear indications that the Long
Parliament differed greatly from its recent predecessors. Previous
parliaments occasionally, even hotly, had criticized the policies of the
king and his ministers, but rarely had offered such formidable challenges to royal prerogatives. Even the Petition of Right simply had
been an attempt to prevent the king from pursuing an unpopular
policy; it had not contested his sovereignty or attempted to curtail his
power. But the Long Parliament challenged the marrow of sovereignty.
Its members inquired into the legality of Ship Money, a decision
already rendered by the courts (although admittedly they had questioned the legality of the decision in Bate's Case), and Parliament
investigated the judges who handed down the decision. Its members
also removed ministers whom the king wished to retain, and, for the
first time in recent English history, they attempted to determine the
length of their deliberation and the frequency of their assembly. In the
magnitude of their departure from recent practice, these actions represented startling developments. Lambert, Russell, and others have
stressed Parliament's historic weakness and timidity. But the more we
stress Parliament's previous weakness and lack of assertiveness, the
more remarkable its actions in the spring of 1641 become.

This was the first reorientation in parliamentary politics. Parliament moved from rather limited objections to royal ministers and
policies that they attributed to those ministers, toward tampering,
albeit reluctantly and in limited ways, with the distribution and
bounds of political authority—although it must be kept in mind that
there was as yet no attack on Charles himself. But, as Kevin Sharpe has
commented recently, "The bill for annual parliaments and the Triennial Act. . . . were products of this radically changed atmosphere. . . .
Never before in early modern England had parliament attempted to
determine its own life or frequency of assembly."[9] The second reorientation came after Charles, fearing mob vengeance against his family,
acquiesced to Strafford's execution.

Strafford's executioners discovered that they had merely substituted
one specter of vengeance for another. Strafford's execution and the
political reorientation of early May by no means alleviated all of their
anxieties. Charles's complicity in the Army Plot revealed an enemy
who was potentially even more dangerous than Strafford.[10] Pym had
perhaps exaggerated the seriousness of the Army Plot, but he had not
invented it. There had been a plot. But it had been difficult enough to

persuade members to condemn a minister like Strafford; even in the wake of the innovative legislation of early May, most members probably still recoiled from a challenge to Charles himself.

In the face of these changing circumstances, the goals of the reform leadership, and even its core, shifted slightly. John Pym, for instance, emerged from the first six months of parliamentary activity with an indifferent record. On the one hand, he could boast of several estimable achievements. First, he had managed to hold together a disparate and contentious body of men over a long and exhaustive period of deliberation. Second, in the panic of early May, he had mustered an impressive body of legislation to thwart the Army Plot and prevent the king from pardoning Strafford. On the other hand, Pym suffered some conspicuous failures. One of his major objectives had been to settle the King's finances, while placing men who held Parliament's trust in high office, and he had failed at both. Furthermore, before May, he enjoyed little legislative success. In February the first major piece of reform legislation, the Triennial Act, had been introduced and promoted by William Strode. Even Pym's grandest undertaking, the impeachment proceedings against Strafford, had to be abandoned, and a bill of attainder advanced in its place. Thus, while Pym could claim several concrete achievements, he clearly could not control the Commons, nor was he any closer to settlement with the King. In fact, with Strafford's blood now on their hands, Pym and the other parliamentary leaders might genuinely fear for their lives.[11]

The position of Oliver St. John as a parliamentary leader, however, improved dramatically in the aftermath of Strafford's trial. St. John opposed impeachment from the first, and he took the lead in justifying the attainder to both the Lords and the Commons.[12] Although the Lords made little use of St. John's arguments in their decision, his reputation was enhanced through the dramatic speech he made to the Lords on 29 April. Sir Symonds D'Ewes reported that the "learned" speech gave "satisfaction to all."[13] Robert Baillie believed that St. John was able to show "in a speech of three hours how the facts proven of Strafford were high treason expressly against many statutes, and answered all the laws seemingly to import the contrarie: and however, no law had made them treason, yet by a number of examples in their law, he showed how the parliament might very legally condone this singular act."[14] On 11 May the Commons had St. John's speech, along with two of Pym's speeches against Strafford, printed as part of a propaganda campaign to ensure the execution.[15] It appears, then, that St. John was perceived by members as playing a key role in securing what was probably the most vital part of the reform program.

The campaign against Strafford also brought Pym and St. John closer together. Contrary to the impression given by Clarendon— who often suggested that Pym, St. John, and others were united in a grand design against the monarchy—as we have seen, there were real and significant differences between the two men. Pym feared primarily a Catholic conspiracy. St. John feared a legal conspiracy. St. John pursued Sir John Finch almost compulsively; Pym tried to save him. St. John believed that the Ship Money decision was at the heart of England's problems; after his opening speech in November 1640, Pym rarely alluded to it. Pym despised anything papist; in a three-hour speech to the Lords about Strafford, St. John never mentioned Catholic plots or even the word papist. Pym, according to Clarendon, was "not of those furious resolutions against the church as the other leading men were"; yet, St. John was the author of the Root and Branch Bill.[16]

Pym and St. John did, however, entertain some key points of contact, which came to be more important than their differences. Both believed that some sort of Godly Reformation was necessary, that the king's erring ministers must be removed, replaced with men capable of holding Parliament's trust, and that the balance of the Ancient Constitution must be restored. Moreover, Pym and St. John possessed two important similarities in temperament, which may have helped push them together. Much recent work on early Stuart history—especially that of Alan Everitt, Derek Hirst, John Morrill, and others—has stressed the need to evaluate the ideas and actions of members of Parliament from a county community perspective. But, as Conrad Russell has observed, our understanding of Pym is not helped by attempting to place him in a local context. Pym did not have a local constituency and was one of the few members who, when they spoke of their country, did not mean their county.[17]

In this respect St. John resembled Pym a great deal. Like Pym, his seat had been secured for him by the earl of Bedford. And, like Pym, he lacked a true local constituency. Neither man really understood the back-bench mentality of most members. Pym was a man devoted to anti-Catholicism and administrative business and finance. St. John was a man devoted to the law. Neither had much interest in the remote world of county politics or the hardy outdoor life of hunting and hawking that commanded the attention of most MPs. As well, Pym and St. John had another affinity that may have helped bring them together, but that, paradoxically, also may have widened the gap between them and the members with strong county community ties. Russell has described Pym as a "good and expeditious man of business who yet somewhat lacked the light touch." In Russell's view, Pym was more determined in his approach to business than any contemporary except Sir Robert Cecil, and in all his adult life he is known to have made only one joke, and that may have been unintentional.[18]

This description could fit St. John as well. We have already quoted Clarendon's description of St. John's stern and forbidding demeanor.[19] As Pym single-mindedly pursued anti-Catholicism and fiscal soundness, so St. John pursued Finch and Ship Money with comparable vigor. Also, like Pym, St. John was known to have made only one joke in his entire career, the odd comparison between war and marriage in his speech on Strafford's attainder.[20] Clearly, men of such reserved natures would find capturing back-bench support a difficult task.

Before his dramatic intervention at the conclusion of Strafford's trial, St. John appears to have been a respected, but largely ineffectual, member of Parliament. His legal expertise was valued and often eagerly sought, but his obsessive emphasis on it stamped him as a one-issue politician. Only a few other members regarded legal issues with the same urgency, and St. John occasionally found himself in conflict with Pym and criticized by other members, usually for his excessive emphasis on legal matters.[21] But, in May 1641, St. John became more decisively involved in parliamentary politics and on a wider spectrum of issues.

The first evidence of a change in St. John's role can be glimpsed in his attempt to help reform the King's finances, an issue that had always been at the center of Pym's policies. Before May, St. John had shown little interest in financial matters and had once successfully obstructed, along with Sir Walter Earle, one of Pym's early tonnage and poundage bills. Nevertheless, in late May, St. John, not Pym, came forward with a new proposal for settling the King's finances.[22] The two-month grant of tonnage and poundage, approved in March, expired in late May, and in the wake of the Army Plot there was still little sympathy to make Charles a lifetime grant. St. John's proposal involved another two-month grant, but one that would turn the money over to the King directly. It also involved coming to terms with the customs farmers, whom many members regarded as delinquent. St. John's proposal promised to yield more revenue without a tax increase because delinquent farmers would be called to a closer accounting. This proposal, however, was opposed bitterly by Strode and Holles, who contended that the money should be controlled by commissioners appointed by Parliament. St. John's seeming advocacy of the royal cause provoked a deeper rancor. Six days later, the Commons gave a first reading to a bill that would debar members of the House from serving the King until they first obtained the consent of both Houses of Parliament, which seemed to be a clear attack on St. John, who remained as the King's solicitor.[23]

St. John's attempt to settle the King's finances in May 1641 seems curious. Why should St. John, of all people, suddenly take an interest in fiscal matters? And why should Pym allow St. John to take the lead? The answers to those questions are complex and, as we shall see, cut across a wide spectrum of issues. Unfortunately, we can only speculate on the answers, because neither Pym nor St. John provided any explanation for their actions. Each man did, however, have some legitimate and obvious reasons for allowing St. John to take charge, if only briefly.

From Pym's point of view, he himself had failed repeatedly to get a settlement on tonnage and poundage, so it was logical for him to let St. John, with his enhanced prestige from the Strafford case, attempt to do so. Anthony Fletcher also has pointed out that Charles's approval of the act against the dissolution of Parliament without its consent on 18 May led to a revival of confidence in the monarchy.[24] Pym could now afford to maneuver a bit in trying to obtain a financial settlement.

From St. John's point of view, his proposals provide evidence of a moderating stance. What he proposed was certainly less than Charles desired, but it was nonetheless more generous to the King than most members wished. But St. John also had several compelling reasons for wishing to appear moderate. As the King's solicitor, St. John had taken a considerable political risk in opposing Strafford, especially in such uncompromising terms. Clarendon, for example, thought that, as solicitor, St. John would be "ashamed to appear in anything prejudicial to the crown."[25] By joining the campaign against Strafford, St. John had certainly been involved in a measure prejudicial to the Crown. Thus, by promoting a measure favorable to the King, St. John may have been attempting to reassure both conservative members and even Charles himself of his continuing respect for the monarchy, and that he was a sober, reflective man of affairs, not a hotheaded radical.

St. John may have had another reason for supporting measures that gave support to the monarchy. He had his own bombshell to drop concerning the bishops. The role of episcopate had been a matter of intense concern to many members since the opening of the Long Parliament. In December 1640 a petition supposedly signed by 15,000 London citizens called for the "Root and Branch" abolition of episcopacy, and in January petitions from thirteen counties expressed similar aims. It was clear, however, that most members, even in the Commons, did not support the wholesale destruction of the episcopate. In the Church debates of February and March, the Commons seemed to be drifting toward a "limited" or "primitive" episcopacy, which would entail reducing the political authority of the bishops while preserving their offices. In March the committee formed to consider ecclesiastical affairs presented a series of proposals designed to create a limited episcopacy. The committee called for the bishops and the clergy to be deprived of all secular offices and employments, including membership in the House of Lords, the Privy Council, the Star Chamber, and other courts. On 1 May a bill to that effect passed the Commons without a single negative vote.[26] Not surprisingly, the Lords chose to reject the Commons's lead. The bishops were an estate of the realm, argued several of the Lords; to expel them at this point might create a dangerous precedent.[27] Accordingly, on 24 May, the Lords passed a resolution affirming the right of the bishops to remain in Parliament. Three days later, on 27 May, Sir Edward Dering introduced a bill, drafted by St. John, for the complete abolition of episcopacy.[28]

Most historians have assumed that the introduction of the Root and Branch bill on 27 May was directly connected to the Lords' resolution of 24 May. Undoubtedly, this view is essentially correct, although several other factors seem to have played a part in its introduction, and the motives of its proponents were far more subtle than has been recognized previously.

The role of St. John in the introduction of the Root and Branch Bill may shed some light on the subtleties involved. St. John had several times in his career evinced some hostility toward the bishops. He was suspected of helping to prepare Henry Burton's defense in 1637, and in the Short Parliament he had argued that innovations in religion could not be imposed solely by convocation of bishops. No canons should be binding, he contended, unless approved by parliament—an argument he continued to advance when the Long Parliament convened.[29] But, in the early stages of the Long Parliament, he was not a vociferous opponent of the bishops. In January 1641, when asked to provide legal justification for the treason charges against the bishops, St. John responded with a tame, almost deferential, comment, far removed from the combative tone of his Ship Money speeches, and neither he nor Pym took much of a role in the bitter February debates on the subject.[30]

At this point, the death of Bedford on 10 May, long recognized by historians as critical to the final collapse of any bridge appointments schemes, may hold a deeper significance. Bedford was not only the political patron and friend of St. John and Pym, he was also an intimate friend of Laud, and a man who, according to Clarendon, had never desired any alteration in the Church. Bedford appears to have been, much more than Pym, the man to whom St. John was closest politically and temperamentally. St. John and Bedford had been on intimate terms since the 1620s. Both had suffered at the hands of the Star Chamber, and both were distressed at the invasions of law by a King who, counseled by self-seeking advisers, did not temper their advice by seeking the wisdom of the great men of the realm.[31] Bedford's moderate stance regarding the Church helped make him acceptable to Charles, and it may also have constrained St. John from being too open about his anti-episcopal views. It is, therefore, probably not a mere coincidence that, less than three weeks after Bedford's death, a bill, written by St. John, was introduced for the abolition of episcopacy. In the debates that followed, St. John made no attempt to conceal his feelings about episcopacy, and his hostility toward the bishops exploded. The bishops had been treasonous since the time of St. Augustine, he declared, and they always had been anti-monarchical.[32] Pym did not exactly lend unqualified support for the Root and Branch Bill, but he did not obstruct it, either. On 3 June he assured members that Root and Branch was a constructive solution and that provisions would be made for bishops whose lands were confiscated.[33]

The May introduction of the Root and Branch Bill was also related to Parliament's need to maintain close and cordial relations with the Scots. Pym's reform policies depended in large part on the continuing presence of a Scottish Army in England. But the Scots were increasingly impatient with schemes to implement a "limited episcopacy." Observing the Commons' debates on the subject, Robert Baillie complained that Parliament's dilatory pace in proceeding with Church reform and its willingness to consider a "limited" episcopacy were simply means to maintain episcopacy as it then stood.[34] By mid-May, Pym and the reformers had to contend with the possibility that Charles might conduct affairs in a manner that would drive a wedge between Parliament and the Covenanters. Charles and James Douglas, marquess of Hamilton, apparently were pursuing this policy, so the news of Charles's impending trip to Scotland was doubly alarming.[35] It was, therefore, imperative in May 1641·that Parliament reassure the Scots of its good faith regarding the settlement of Church affairs, and the most expeditious way to accomplish this aim was to propose legislation for Church reform of the English Church along the Presbyterian model. Such action, of course, while placating the Scots and raising the hopes of the extreme opponents of episcopacy would offend the conservatives in the Commons as well as most of the Lords although St. John's financial bill might have served to reassure them of the moderate aims of the reformers.

It is possible, then, that the introduction of a financial bill in May 1641 and the introduction of the Root and Branch Bill are connected. Taken together, they represented a shrewd tactical maneuver that might solve temporarily the leadership's principal problems. First, after a highly charged period of time—which had seen Strafford tried and executed, the Protestation subscribed, and the act against the dissolution of Parliament passed—Pym and St. John may have needed a device, like the tonnage and poundage bill, to reassure the conservative majority in the Commons of their good intentions toward the monarchy. Second, the possible defection of the Scots posed a still graver danger to the reformers, and the introduction of the Root and Branch Bill served to reassure the Scots that Parliament was pursuing a religious settlement of which they would approve. It probably did not matter to Pym or St. John that there was little chance that either measure would pass at this point; their real value was in the impression they would make. For St. John the matter of impression was especially important. Although he had opposed Strafford vehemently, he undoubtedly wished to retain his position as the king's solicitor. Advancing the tonnage and poundage bill made him appear more loyal to the monarchy, and—even in the matter of Root and Branch— he attacked the bishops far more for what he perceived as their treasonous capacity and anti-monarchical tendencies than for any spiritual deficiency.

The reorientation of May 1641 probably held more significance for St. John than for Pym. By acting in concert with Pym, St. John had moved into the inner circle of parliamentary leadership, and, for the first time, he had emerged as more than a one-issue politician. His political vision had been expanded to include matters of finance and religion as well as the law. He was no longer simply a persistent voice insisting that Charles's behavior before the beginning of the Bishops' Wars suggested a tendency toward arbitrary government and an unwillingness to work through Parliament. Moreover, the man who had not been willing to compromise on Ship Money, Finch, or Strafford now appeared willing to enter the dissembling and subtle world of political infighting. And he perfected, in May 1641, two techniques for political infighting that he would employ again and again as his political career progressed. As we have seen, he promoted at some risk a measure (tonnage and poundage) favorable to the king, just before he was involved in a measure (Root and Branch) that Charles was certain to oppose. And St. John, while drafting the controversial measure himself, had it introduced by someone else. Later, in November 1641, while members debated the Grand Remonstrance, St. John took little part in the debate. Instead, he pushed tirelessly for the renewal of tonnage and poundage. But, in early December, he drafted a Militia Bill intended to take power from the King, and—just as Sir Edward Dering introduced the Root and Branch Bill, written by St. John—Sir Arthur Haselrig introduced the Militia Bill.[36] In 1643, St. John, an opponent of the earl of Essex, used his friend, Samuel Browne, to suggest that Essex's friend, the earl of Holland, be impeached for treason. Essex, not deceived, moved that St. John, not Browne, be impeached instead.[37] And, in 1645, while engaged in the reform of the army, St. John initiated the final proceedings against Laud to persuade the Scots of his good faith in religion, knowing that the Scots did not favor the reforms that he and Vane proposed.[38]

It must be admitted, however, that, legislatively, St. John's brief tenure was a failure. Neither the financial reforms nor Root and Branch succeeded. St. John was no more successful in obtaining a settlement than Pym was. In terms of political posturing, however, he may have been more successful. He remained an active force in the parliamentary leadership during the summer and fall of 1641, but he apparently never offended Charles as deeply as some of the other opposition leaders did. In January 1642, when Charles arrived at Westminster to arrest the Five Members, St. John was not one of them, even though his record as a combative opponent of royal policy was comparable to several of those Charles tried to arrest. He had apparently already mastered the ability to play on both sides without offending the other. This ability was, however, a predilection that would come back to haunt him in the later stages of the revolution.

In addition to religious and fiscal reforms, the Commons addressed several other pressing matters in the summer of 1641. Many members were determined to destroy the perceived instruments of royal tyranny during the Personal Rule and to compel Charles to rule under strict constitutional limitations. On 8 June 1641 bills for the abolition of the Courts of Star Chamber and High Commission were read a third time without a division. On the same day John Selden brought in three additional bills.[39] One declared that Ship Money was illegal; a second limited the extent of the royal forests; and a third abolished knighthood fees.

Surprisingly, St. John said little on these matters, even concerning Ship Money. On 23 June he attacked knights' fees as excessive, remarking in a phrase that summed up his political philosophy that he and his colleagues did "not intend by this bill to take away the King's ancient right but only the abuse."[40] A week later, on 30 June 1641, he complained about men being falsely arrested in the forests.[41]

St. John's most striking comments concerned the Star Chamber. On 7 July, St. John delivered a message to the Commons from the King, who asked that the Commons give special consideration to officers of the Star Chamber because, Charles contended, they had accepted governmental office at considerable cost to their personal fortunes. The next day St. John vigorously took up the king's position. Although conceding that the Star Chamber had performed illegal acts, he reminded members that it was a court established by law and that it was the judges who pronounced on the law, not the officers of the court, and it was the judges' malfeasances that should concern them. (Finch had fled, but St. John had not forgotten him.) St. John then suggested that Star Chamber officials who lost their jobs should be compensated and that a committee should be formed to investigate.[42]

In his *History,* Clarendon bitterly derided St. John for accepting the post of King's Solicitor and then failing to promote the king's interests.[43] There is little doubt that St. John—despite his periodic differences of opinion with Pym, Holles, and others of the Commons' leadership—continued to identify with those opposed to aspects of royal policy. On two key issues, Strafford's attainder and the Root and Branch Bill, St. John clearly departed from the interests of the king. Yet, Clarendon's sardonic assessment does not tell the entire story. St. John remained behind the scenes in the Strafford case until it began to collapse. As we have seen, in May 1641 he tried to assemble a compromise that would have produced a settlement financially favorable to the king. Finally, in July 1641, we can see him supporting another aspect of the King's business in the debates over the Star Chamber. Clarendon was correct to view St. John as a less than committed royal servant, but, as we shall see in the next chapter as well, unqualified acceptance of this view is misleading.

The debates on these bills, the so-called "constructive legislation" of the summer of 1641, occasionally were interrupted by emergency matters. The first emergency arose in the frenzy surrounding the Second Army Plot in June 1641, which provided further indications that Charles was prepared to use military force against Parliament. Revelation of this plot triggered yet another wave of anti-Catholic hysteria. The Commons's debate was so violent and emotional that the usually circumspect Lenthall confessed that he feared for his life.[44] For the first time St. John was caught in the swelling anti-Catholic feeling. On 17 June the judges of the King's Bench sent a message to the Commons that William O'Connor, an Irish priest who had threatened to shoot the king, could not be condemned for treason because his accusers could produce only one witness to the treasonous words. St. John then launched into a lengthy diatribe against O'Connor and the judges, arguing that some means should be found to convict O'Connor, although St. John did not specify how the two-witness rule should be circumvented.[45]

The Second Army Plot also convinced parliamentary leaders to abandon, at least for the moment, the debate about Church governance and address matters of safety instead. Pym's solution to the Army Plot and Charles's unwillingness to recognize the need for acceptable counsel was the Ten Propositions, which Pym persuaded Parliament to accept on 24 June. A searing indication of how deeply Charles was still mistrusted, the Ten Propositions asked the king to postpone his departure to Scotland until both the English and Scottish Armies could be disbanded, to bar all Catholics from the court, and to replace his present ministers with "such officers and councellors as his people and Parliament may have just cause to confide in."[46] In essence, the Ten Propositions asked Charles to accept several components of the May 1641 compromise schemes without the financial settlement and without assurance that assaults on the Church would be discontinued. Under these circumstances, it is probably not surprising that Charles refused to sign the Ten Propositions.

By early August the parliamentary leadership must have experienced a mounting sense of exasperation and frustration. Strafford had been executed; other ministers were either in prison or in flight; the Triennial Act, the Act against dissolving Parliament without its own consent, and the "constructive legislation" of the summer of 1641 had all been passed; and yet settlement stood further away than ever. The events of May had forced the leadership to forsake the bridge appointments scheme. Plots and rumors of plots still abounded and were taken seriously by members, and yet Charles rejected the Ten Propositions. In June, Secretary Vane had remarked sadly, "We are still here in the labyrinth and cannot get out."[47] It was still true at the end of July.

4

The Coming of the Civil War

Since May, Charles had made clear his intention to visit Scotland in order to conclude a peace treaty with the Scots, and his efforts to negotiate with the Scots continued throughout the summer of 1641. If concluded, such a treaty would mean the disbanding of the Scots' army, which would deprive Parliament of its principal instrument of leverage. It was also possible, although in hindsight not likely, that Charles could persuade the Scots to ally with him by offering them a religious settlement more in accordance with their wishes than Parliament's.

St. John feared Charles's northern journey enough that he appears to have participated in a brief attempt to use tonnage and poundage as a bargaining chip to dissuade Charles from going. In June, Charles had finally signed the act, passed by Parliament in May, which placed tonnage and poundage under parliamentary control. Although his predecessors had enjoyed customs duties for life, Charles was now forced to request the money from Parliament, and it was granted to him only for brief, specified periods of time. The first grant became effective on 20 May and expired on 15 July, at which time another bill was passed.[1]

On two occasions in early August, St. John suggested that an early renewal of tonnage and poundage be made, even though a second grant had been approved on 12 July. Observing the discussion, D'Ewes remarked that members decided to lay the bill aside, while suggesting that they might want to take it up again should the King decide to postpone his trip to Scotland.[2]

This incident suggests that St. John and others still thought, as many of them had in May, that money could be used as a lever against the King. But, like his attempt to secure financial bills for the King in May, this apparent scheme to use tonnage and poundage to persuade the king to postpone his trip to Scotland failed.

On 10 August, Charles finally signed an agreement with the Scots. The terms included a provision that Parliament raise £300,000 to compensate the Scots for their losses in three years in the field. The

Scots also demanded that £80,000 be paid to them immediately, and, in July, Parliament had already passed a Poll Tax to raise some of the money.[3] In August, with the treaty concluded, Parliament petitioned Charles to delay his trip, but Charles rejected the petition, and he arrived in Edinburgh on 14 August.

While members continued to express concern about Charles's intentions in Scotland, they also used his absence to make further encroachments on his power. Pym convinced both houses to adopt a resolution dispatching their own commissioners to Scotland "to preserve good relations between the two kingdoms." The commissioners were essentially parliamentary watchdogs. Six members, all oppositionists, including Hampden and Fiennes, were selected. Their charge was to inform the two houses of activity concerning the welfare of the two kingdoms.[4]

Despite the urgency that accompanied affairs with Scotland, interest in matters of State sometimes lagged. Members had been sitting since November 1640 without recess. Boredom, fear of a recent outbreak of the plague, and homesickness reduced the attendance in the Commons to fewer than seventy during the last week in August. In Pym's mind, continued sitting meant the possibility of losing his fragile consensus. Some sort of recess was necessary.

On the other hand, with Charles in Scotland, there were palpable risks in taking a recess. Charles, unpredictable and untrustworthy, might attempt a countermove in Parliament's absence. To circumvent such a possibility, Parliament on 9 September created a committee consisting of forty-seven members of the Commons and seventeen members of the Lords, to manage business during the recess. The committee's members included Pym, St. John, Strode, and the younger Vane. Specifically, the committee's task was to demobilize the English Army and issue directions in Parliament's name to the commissioners in Scotland. Several members objected to the provision giving the committee power to direct the commissioners in Scotland, but St. John defended its necessity, and the bill passed without modifications.[5]

Whereas this committee solved the immediate problems of the leadership, Pym and St. John faced still more serious obstacles. In ten months of deliberations Parliament had secured some important reforms and had obtained some remarkable concessions. But it stood farther away than ever from an agreement with Charles. The King still refused to confer ministerial office on Pym or his friends, and he was coming increasingly to believe that Pym and his friends were committed to their own self-serving conspiracy against him. Other ominous signs loomed. To many in the localities the constitutional gains of the spring and summer of 1641 were less significant than the fact that they were accompanied by several new taxes, including the Poll Tax, which fell on every householder. The acerbic Yorkshire gentlewoman Margaret Eure complained, "I am in such a great rage with Parliament as nothing will pacify me, for they promised us all should be well, if my Lord Strafford's head were off, and since then there is nothing better, but I think we shall be undone with taxes." Moreover, several members began to see the wisdom behind the argument that, whatever their faults, the bishops should be retained as an essential link in the chain of hierarchy and order. Disorders in Kent, for example, drove Sir Edward Dering, the man who introduced the Root and Branch Bill in May, to abandon his support for it.[6]

Some of the complaints about Parliament specifically cited Pym and St. John. A widely circulated pamphlet, *The Protestants' Protestation,* named Pym, Hampden, Holles, Haselrig, St. John, and others in the Commons—along with "Saye the Anabaptist," Essex, Mandeville, Warwick, and others among the Lords—as the "perpetrators of a conspiracy against the King, Crown, and posterity." Pym, St. John, and the others stood accused of prostituting the honor of England by "beggaring" the nation to the Scots and destroying all freedom of speech in Parliament. The petition concluded by accusing Pym and his allies of protecting "the ignorant and licentious sectaries and schismatics to stir up sedition, to bring in atheism, discountenance all reverend ministers and take away the prayerbook."[7]

When Parliament reassembled on 20 October, the *Protestation* was an immediate subject of concern, but members soon turned to other, more urgent matters. In early October several of Charles's newfound Scottish supporters attempted to seize two of their leading opponents, Archibald Campbell, the earl of Argyle, and Hamilton. The seizure, which came to be known as "the Incident," was bungled, and Charles once again was implicated in an episode that reinforced parliamentary suspicions of a Royalist conspiracy just as Parliament was about to resume its deliberations.

Even with the opportunity handed them by the Incident, the leadership faced a nasty dilemma. Any successful reform campaign depended on increased cooperation and support from the House of Lords. On the other hand, the Lords had been an obstacle to the Commons' plans, and if the bishops could be denied their seats among the Lords, reform might proceed more easily. To this end, St. John entered the renewal of the debate on the bishops' exclusion, arguing that the bishops were not part of the traditional balanced government of the One, the Few, and the Many. Although St. John was probably incorrect in this assertion, he added what amounted to a compromise, by suggesting that anyone who resigned from "Holy Orders" ought to be eligible for secular employments and offices. This suggestion aroused the immediate rancor of D'Ewes, who contended that many who had entered the holy orders had done so only to "swallow up and possess the great revenues of our church," and, if allowed to enter secular offices, they would display the same tendencies. St. John tried again on 27 October, this time omitting the section regarding the bishops' eligibility for secular appointments.[8] Compromise was not always the proper path to legislative success.

Debate on the bishops' exclusion was interrupted by the cataclysmic news of the outbreak of a rebellion in Ireland. News of the rebellion reached Charles on the links at Leith on 27 October and was officially transmitted to Parliament on 1 November. All at once, news of the rebellion in Ireland vindicated Pym's program and seemingly gave a terrifying credence to the perceived popish menace. The possibility of Irish Catholic rebels invading English territory and property raised as terrifying a specter as any English citizen could conceive.[9] The proper response to the rebellion soon became a critical issue. Many members believed that an army should be raised to subdue the rebels. But, legally, only the King could do this. Could Parliament, in the wake of army plots and the Incident, trust him to raise the army? Moreover, Charles had not yet returned from Scotland.

In Pym's mind the rebellion immediately raised again the question of the King's counselors. Clearly for him, Charles could not be given an army unless men who inspired Parliament's trust and confidence were given command. St. John supported a more moderate solution, lending support to a proposal on 5 November that Scottish troops be hired to subdue the rebellion. This solution would place command in anti-Catholic hands with leaders whom Parliament could trust without challenging Charles's authority directly.[10] But before anything could be concluded, Pym came forward on 5 November with a truly revolutionary proposal: unless evil counselors were removed, the Commons would be forced, "by discharge of the trust which we owe to the state, and those we represent to resolve some way of defending Ireland." This controversial measure passed the Commons 151–110, and the house thereby professed its willingness to proceed without the king and to use its responsibility to the nation as a justification.[11]

On 8 November, Pym introduced a new measure, the Grand Remonstrance, into the lower house. A committee, which included St. John, had been formed in November 1640 to prepare a precise statement on Parliament's grievances.[12] But, given members' preoccupation with the drama of Strafford, the Root and Branch Bill, and the legislation of the summer of 1641, the Remonstrance project had been laid aside. The House of Commons had several times asked the committee to submit its work, but no document appeared before the September recess, suggesting either that it was not finished or that Pym was simply waiting for the proper moment to release it.

Confronted with the Irish threat, Pym and the others may have decided to bring the Remonstrance forward as a device to extract some guarantee from Charles that the army in Ireland would be commanded by men who retained Parliament's confidence. The Remonstrance was a list of every offense, both real and imagined, committed by Charles and his advisers. Perhaps by overwhelming Charles with the staggering list of Parliament's grievances, Pym hoped to persuade the King to allow Parliament to select the army's commanders. As well, Pym undoubtedly intended the Remonstrance as a propaganda device to remind members now turning away from the leadership that Charles and his advisers still had much to answer for.

On seven different occasions between 9 and 23 November, the House of Commons discussed the Remonstrance. On 22 November a fierce debate continued until after midnight. If Pym believed that the Remonstrance would generate more support for his policies, he was mistaken. With its insinuations of distrust and pretentions of forcing the king's compliance, the Remonstrance further divided members of Parliament. "When I first heard of a Remonstrance," said Sir Edward Dering, "I did not dream that we should remonstrate downward, tell stories to the people, and talk of the king as a third person." An angry Sir John Culpepper declared that "this is a Remonstrance of the people. Remonstrances ought to be sent to the King for redress. . . . We are not sent here to please the people." Emotions soared to high levels on both sides. A distressed D'Ewes left the house when the debates became particularly intense. In the end the Remonstrance passed 159–148 after an angry debate that culminated with the drawing of swords in the house.[13] Oliver Cromwell later remarked that if the Remonstrance had failed he would have left England. An equally divisive debate then erupted over whether or not the Remonstrance should be printed.

St. John was remarkably quiet during the debates on the Remonstrance, but, nonetheless, he may have been working toward his own solution. As early as 12 November he reminded members that the August grant of tonnage and poundage expired December 1, and a committee considering the book of rates needed to meet that afternoon.[14] On 25 November, St. John, expressing some irritation at the failure of the committee to fix a book of rates, and fearing that the present bill would expire before a new one could be passed, brought in his own bill.[15] On the 27th he made another financial proposal, reviving a bill for the granting of eight subsidies by the clergy that had been discussed several times in previous months without resolution. St. John again encountered resistance, as D'Ewes commented: "Others spake to it, but it was laid aside for the present."[16] On 29 November the Tonnage and Poundage bill was finally passed, but when St. John moved that it be sent up to the Lords, others, according to D'Ewes, opposed it. Those opposing did not want to present the bill until the Lords had accepted amendments to their bill for securing recusants. Eventually, however, after a nomination from D'Ewes, St. John carried the bill to the Lords, although D'Ewes refused to go with him.[17]

The difficulty that St. John encountered with tonnage and poundage was again similar to the opposition Pym had encountered with his financial bills. With the Irish crisis still unremedied, many members must have been reluctant to allow the King more money. However, as in May, St. John may have been using tonnage and poundage, first, to prove his loyalty as a royal servant; and second, perhaps because as in May, he had his own bombshell to drop.

The King returned to London 25 November amidst widespread, almost delirious, celebration and with Parliament no closer to a decision regarding Ireland. On 27 November a bill introduced by William Strode called for placing "the kingdom in a posture of defense," and it generated almost dead silence. Perhaps impatient with the delay, St. John took charge, drafting a militia bill that was introduced by Sir Arthur Haselrig on 7 December.[18] As in almost everything in which St. John was involved during the Long Parliament, his motives remain cloudy, and the meaning of his actions ambiguous. The bill empowered a lord general to raise and command the militia, to levy money to pay it, and to execute martial law. The bill also specified an admiral's place, but blanks were left in the spaces provided for the admiral and the lord general. Several members, including Sir John Culpepper, wanted the bill cast out because assembling the proposed militia was the king's prerogative. St. John was prepared with a vigorous defense, declaring that power ought to be entrusted to someone in the event of an invasion, that present law on this question was unclear, and that Parliament had every right to nominate persons of trust. These men, St. John continued, in yet another burst of conciliatory phrasing, might well be the king's own men, and he hoped that they would be so.[19] St. John apparently even visited Charles in an attempt to persuade him that this was a moderate bill, and that Charles should state his support at least for settling the Irish question before Parliament. Clarendon later interpreted this move as an attempt to trick Charles into supporting the bill.[20]

If one takes St. John's words on a surface level of meaning, they seem reasonable, even moderate. In the highly charged atmosphere of December 1641, however, Parliament was not likely to approve of the "King's men" unless they were also Parliament's men. Fears of Charles's capacity for revenge still lingered in the men who had sent Strafford to his death.

If Charles had then suggested that the earl of Essex should be appointed to command in Ireland, he might have deflected the main thrust of the Militia Bill, dispelled the climate of distrust on which his enemies (especially Pym) depended, and won over members leaning in his direction. Nevertheless, Charles continued to destroy his position, compounding his previous mistakes with a fresh series of blunders in December 1641. Even the Lords rejected his appointment on 22 December of the notorious and disreputable Thomas Lunsford to command of the Tower. One day later, Charles announced his rejection of the Grand Remonstrance. On 27 December, Charles proposed that the Lords raise ten thousand volunteers for Ireland who would be placed under his command, and, on 1 January 1642, he appointed Culpepper and Falkland to high office when he might have reassured wavering members by appointing Pym or Hampden. All during the last week of December, unruly crowds roamed around Westminster, battling local authorities and shouting insults at the bishops, Lunsford, and the Lords. The crowds were frightening enough to lead one of the bishops, John Williams—along with eleven others—to declare that all proceedings in the upper house were void until the bishops' safety could be ensured. This declaration raised the question of whether Parliament could exist without them. In response the Commons decided to impeach Williams and his supporters and sent them to the Tower. It is not surprising, therefore, that Thomas Coke spoke of the saddest and most tumultous Christmas that "in all my life I ever yet knew."[21]

On 31 December, a Friday, an emotional debate continued over measures for Ireland. Pym, Holles, Strode, and others worked on a new resolution over the weekend. On Monday, 3 January, they were surprised to hear rumors that Charles was about to resort to desperate measures. Reacting to other rumors that the House of Commons was contemplating proceedings against the queen, and encouraged by an emotional Lord Digby, Charles prepared to arrest Pym, Holles, Hampden, Strode, and Haselrig for treason. On 3 January 1642 he sent the Lords a notice of impeachment charges against the "Five Members" and Viscount Mandeville, fully expecting the Lords' approval. The Lords, however, delayed, and Charles arrived at Westminster the next day with several hundred armed men intending to arrest them himself. But, alerted by other members, his victims had fled. Members in both houses were stunned; Charles had demonstrated his untrustworthiness at just the time when he needed to appear worthy of trust, and he had indicated his willingness to use force against Parliament. On 10 January, Charles, against the advice of Essex, evacuated London, not to return until 1648 when he faced his trial and execution.

St. John's absence from the list of "Five Members" is at once surprising and understandable. He did not have the history of opposition that Pym, Hampden, Holles, and Strode had. But his career in the Long Parliament paralleled Haselrig's. Both had pushed for Strafford's attainder, opposed the bishops, and promoted the Militia Bill. It is possible to see St. John's absence from the list as a testament to his political skills. St. John had advocated and supported most of the radical legislation of the Lord Parliament. Yet, he appears to have successfully played both sides by his push for tonnage and poundage and his occasional professions of the loyalty to the Crown.

In the days after the attempt on the Five Members, an air of heroic excitement swirled around London. On 11 January the Five Members returned to London, welcomed by exuberant cheering and cries of encouragement. A thousand horsemen rode into London from Buckinghamshire, John Hampden's home county, proclaiming their willingness to die for the parliamentary cause. At varying intervals over the next few weeks, Charles made a number of conciliatory gestures, indicating his willingness to work with Parliament on militia appointments, to discuss aspects of the Grand Remonstrance, and to withdraw the charges against the Five Members.[22]

Unfortunately for Charles, these gestures, which might have won him overwhelming support in December, now were ineffectual. Charles's position, both ideologically and within Parliament, was by no means insupportable, but member after member in January 1642 rose to deplore Charles's breach of privilege. For his part, Charles was increasingly persuaded that he was being destroyed by a "malignant party" determined to destroy him for its own selfish ends.[23]

Charles still retained a solid opportunity to recover his losses, because many members were torn between conflicting loyalties and passions. St. John was one of these members. While Parliament was debating Charles's breach of privilege, additional rumors flourished around Westminster that additional charges might be preferred against St. John and Sir Walter Earle, as well as Brooke, Essex, Saye, and Warwick among the Lords.[24]

St. John behaved as though he feared both a royal and a parliamentary reprisal. He said little as the Commons deliberated about the attempt on the Five Members. But on 15 January, responding to consideration of the treason charges against Sir Edward Herbert for preferring charges against the Five Members, the man who had once justified Strafford's attainder on the grounds that he resembled a beast of prey, no more entitled to law than wolves or foxes who could be killed just as they are found, argued that it was one thing if Herbert performed this action on his own initiative and another if he was compelled by the King to prefer the charges.[25] St. John found support from Sir Henry Vane, but few others. He also moved to prevent Holles from examining the indictment of Gregory Dexter, a printer charged with treason.[26]

The dramatic events of January 1642 did not lead St. John to forget about tonnage and poundage. On 20 January he moved that a day should be set aside for consideration of a book of rates because the present tonnage and poundage bill would expire in about ten days.[27] Following this motion, the Commons requested a report from the committee of customers on the following Monday. On 26 January, St. John proposed a bill for an extended grant of tonnage and poundage and found himself under comprehensive attack. Sir Henry Vane the Younger, supported by D'Ewes, objected to the bill and suggested again the need to pass a two-month grant. William Purefoy then asked whether it was proper for a member to bring in a bill without a special request from the house. St. John responded angrily that it was his sense of the Commons that consideration of a book of rates indicated that the house was prepared to consider a bill regarding tonnage and poundage.[28] D'Ewes thought that the matter should be laid aside for the moment, but Pym, Holles, and others, "moving with great violence," attacked the bill and St. John himself for proposing a subsidy without special authority from the house. Chastened, on 27 January, St. John brought in a bill for a limited grant of tonnage and poundage, which was approved on 29 January.[29]

Here, St. John apparently was trying again to cover himself on both sides. Proposing a lifetime grant of tonnage and poundage might prove his loyalty to the Crown. But St. John also protected himself from a potential parliamentary reprisal by dropping hints that, as a royal servant, he had been forced by the King to put up the lifetime grant. As D'Ewes remarked, "I learned afterwards that he [St.John] was commanded by his majesty to bring in this bill . . . the crafty solicitor, whom I thought very honest, and I spoke about this very thing freely and boldly."[30] And, of course, he had earlier planted the idea that a royal servant might be compelled to do things against his wishes on the King's orders in reference to the debate on Edward Herbert.

St. John also seems to have offered little support to Pym's efforts to break the parliamentary deadlock. Since October the House of Lords had resisted both attempts at the bishops' exclusion and the demand that the King surrender his authority over the militia. Clearly, the two propositions were linked: if the bishops could be expelled from the Lords, the loss of their votes might be enough to secure passage of the Militia Bill. Petitions from many counties and speeches from Pym and Holles warned of the collapse of trade, widespread unemployment, and the desperation to which the poor might be driven under these circumstances. Under the pressure of Pym's attack and fears of popular disturbance, the Lords caved in. On 1 February they accepted the Commons' demand to the King for parliamentary control of the militia. Four days later, they passed a bill expelling the bishops. On 15 February they passed the Militia Bill itself. The Lords had thus surrendered their position as a buffer between the Commons and the King.[31]

At the same time, Charles made several attempts to display good faith in his relations with Parliament. He appointed Parliament's nominee, Sir John Conyers, as lieutenant of the Tower, and he gave his consent to the bill against the secular employments of the clergy. Charles, however, was apparently just playing for time until he could be certain that the queen was safely away from England, as he postponed his reply to the Militia Bill until after her departure for Holland on 23 February.[32] His rejection of the Militia Ordinance of 28 February produced another crisis. With Pym exerting his influence on both the Lords and the Commons, both houses swiftly rejected the King's reply. The petition from the Commons, which called Charles a "hazard to the peace and safety of the kingdom," compelled D'Ewes, deeply troubled by the proceedings, to withdraw from the house. Charles returned an equally intransigent answer to the parliamentary petition, and on 2 March both houses voted to put the kingdom into a state of defense by means of the militia. On 5 March they passed the ordinance, specified the names of the Lords lieutenant, and denied the legitimacy of all previous commissions of array issued by the king.[33]

Surprisingly, for a man so powerfully involved in previous controversial matters, St. John remained largely silent during these often-angry debates. He did not make any recorded comments about the Five Members, and only Whitelock remarked on his support for the Militia Ordinance.[34] Instead, St. John engaged in several relatively minor skirmishes with D'Ewes and Holles. On 19 February, St. John and D'Ewes debated whether evidence concerning the bishops could be heard without a lord steward present. Both St. John and D'Ewes agreed that such evidence was admissible without the presence of a lord steward; they contested the reason why it was. On 21 February, St. John and Holles discussed the proper way to proceed against the bishops. Holles wanted a bill drawn up immediately with charges outlined in a general manner; St. John wanted the proofs heard and discussed before proceeding to a bill.[35]

Between December 1641 and March 1642, St. John seems to have become more moderate at a time when the issues dividing the king and Parliament were becoming more evident. From one angle of vision he appears to have labored resolutely to plant his feet firmly on both sides of the fence. Perhaps alarmed by the arrest of the Five Members and the further rumors that charges might be preferred against him, St. John may have advanced his proposal for a lifetime grant of tonnage and poundage to provide himself with a defense in case of a royal coup d'état. On the other hand, he also planted the idea that a royal servant could be absolved from action by Parliament if the royal servant had acted on kingly command. St. John also was skillful enough at rumor mongering to plant his ideas in such a way that D'Ewes, keeping a record of these proceedings, heard about them.

The quarrel regarding the militia underscored almost every debate over the following two months. During the course of the debate parliamentary arguments advanced from demands for the removal of certain derelict ministers and odious impositions to demands for change in the nature and structure of government itself. In late March, Charles journeyed north, hoping to muster popular support and vaguely entertaining the idea of seizing the garrison at Hull. On 23 April, Sir John Hotham, the parliamentary governor at Hull, refused to admit him, and Charles issued an angry protest. Equally indignant, a parliamentary declaration challenged the "erroneous maxim, being infused into princes, that their kingdoms are their own, and that they may do with them what they will." Executive power, the petition continued, was only "entrusted to him, for the good and safety and best advantage of the nation, as this trust is for the use of the kingdom, so it ought to be managed by the advice of the houses of Parliament."[36] On 6 June in the petition defending the Militia Ordinance, Parliament declared that its ideas now possessed "the stamp of the royal authority," and that royal pleasure "is declared in this high court of law and counsel after a more eminent and obligatory manner than it can be by personal act or resolution of his own."[37]

St. John continued to be relatively silent as the propaganda war accelerated, although there is no way to know if he contributed to the drafting of Parliament's manifestos and declarations. In any event he did not play the conspicuous role that he played in the late spring and early summer of 1641. St. John's role diminished further as the summer of 1642 passed and civil war loomed nearer. He also exhibited considerable confusion about what his proper role should be. In May 1642, when Lord Keeper Littleton fled to York with the Great Seal, St. John offered the controversial proposal that a new Great Seal be made. Before Littleton's flight Parliament had been claiming that, because it had the Great Seal, none of the King's actions or proclamations had any authority. St. John's proposal aroused some antipathy, but it eventually passed, and, in November 1643, St. John was appointed one of the commissioners for the Great Seal.[38]

After making his bold and astonishing proposal regarding the Great Seal, St. John then appeared to retreat into a more timid stance. In June 1642, St. John asked the Commons if he should obey the King's command to join him in York on the raising of the royal standard.[39] The Commons refused him leave to go, but it is surprising that St. John felt compelled to ask. Was his request to the Commons just another attempt to cover his tracks? Did St. John use the King's request as a ploy to create legal protection for himself in case the rebellion backfired? This ploy seems quite likely. If the rebellion backfired and St. John was later asked why he remained with Parliament, he could now reply that he had been ordered to stay by Parliament.

This episode also indicates St. John's ability and willingness to look toward the future and prepare for possible changes in the course of events. St. John's inclination along this line also can be seen in the fall of 1642. In August 1642 the Scottish General Assembly sent a congenial message to Parliament, anticipating a future alliance between the Scots and Parliament and urging the speedy destruction of episcopacy as the first step toward cementing that union.[40] On 1 September the Commons debated the Scots' message. Overwhelming opposition to the bishops was immediately evident. While member after member assailed the bishops, however, St. John interrupted the debate, insisting that the matter be postponed at least until the following Sunday. D'Ewes expressed great surprise at St. John's request, coming, as he noted, from a man whom many regarded as a radical Puritan.[41] D'Ewes's surprise is understandable. As we have seen, St. John drafted the Root and Branch Bill and made several powerful speeches against episcopacy. But, as Valerie Pearl pointed out some years ago, there were sound political reasons to delay a decision on the bishops. First, at some point Parliament was going to have to negotiate with the Scots, and if it abolished episcopacy it would surrender a critical bargaining chip without getting any comparable Scottish concession in return. Second, as St. John pointed out himself in a debate in December 1642, transfer of the bishops' lands might also hinder

future negotiations with Charles.[42] Two of St. John's political charac-
teristics become evident from these remarks. First, he was not a man
blindly committed to the destruction of the Church. Clearly, he
wanted it accomplished at the most favorable moment to gain political concessions. Second, by supporting the retention of episcopacy, St.
John demonstrated his ability to perceive the larger pattern of events
and to anticipate changes, and his recognition of the fact that a day of
reckoning with the King or the Scots would arrive.

In the fall of 1642, St. John also found himself in a conflict with
Holles that to a degree foreshadowed their future clashes.[43] In November, St. John wanted to introduce Parliament's latest peace proposals with a preamble that would provide a justification for previous
parliamentary actions. Holles, D'Ewes, and others opposed St. John,
arguing that his proposal amounted to a "ripping up of old sores
which ought rather to be skinned and healed." Holles later added that
Parliament should proceed against no more than two Royalists, and
that it need not continue supporting the Militia Ordinance.[44] St.
John's response to these remarks with Holles (i.e., his desire for a
rigorous settlement with the King and Holles's desire for swift settlement) was readily apparent in the fall of 1642.

Despite the intensity and fervor behind some of the parliamentary
debates, the leadership in the Commons did not drift easily into civil
war. Several historians have reminded us recently that the English
Civil War broke out sporadically and lethargically, and that it was a
war that almost no one wanted.[45] Many members either sought
refuge in neutralism or displayed considerable confusion about their
roles. St. John was clearly trying frenetically to hedge his bets and to
provide himself with an escape route should the rebellion collapse. St.
John's schemes and dissimulations, however, should not cause us to
forget that he did choose the parliamentary side, and that, once the
Civil War broadened into a large-scale conflict, he directed all his
energies toward achieving a decisive victory.

5
The Reign of King John

The outbreak of civil war in October 1642 blew a cold blast of reality on many members of Parliament; they had finally fired on the King. This realization appalled some members, and a group of them, led by Denzil Holles, called for a quick settlement with the King. Another group was delighted by the onset of hostilities. The "war party" wing of Parliament, led by the Republican Henry Marten, demanded still bolder and more decisive moves against the King.

At one time, historians believed that early civil war politics could be understood in terms of this war/peace party split. But in the aftermath of Edgehill there appears to have existed a group of hybrid MPs who seemingly defied easy classification. Led in spirit by John Pym, these men, such as John Clotworthy and John Glynn, supported measures proposed by both groups.[1] The outlook of this group was moderate and best expressed in the Grand Remonstrance and the Nineteen Propositions. The members who identified with the middle group steadfastly upheld the Constitution and the monarchy, but they believed that specific limitations on the monarch must be implemented to preserve the Constitution.[2]

It must be remembered that Pym never actually formed or organized a middle group; he simply steered a middle course that attracted majority support. In fact, none of the parliamentary groups, not even the "war" and "peace" parties, was a self-conscious, corporate body, maintaining a formal structure or organization. It also may be possible, as Valerie Pearl has argued, to extend the life of the middle group beyond Pym's death in 1643, whereupon informal leadership was assumed by Oliver St. John.[3]

There is little doubt that, beginning in the summer of 1643, St. John's career took another dramatic turn, as he finally assumed the powerful role for which he seemed to be destined in the summer and fall of 1641. St. John's first involvement in post-Edgehill politics, the Solemn League and Covenant with the Scots, involved negotiations on very delicate religious and political issues. By the summer of 1643, Pym regarded military assistance from the Scots to be imperative. For their part, the Scots—fearing that Charles might employ Irish soldiers against them—came to see their own interests served by the alliance, and, in the summer of 1643, Pym—assisted by St. John and Vane— concluded an agreement with the Scots, the Solemn League and Covenant.[4]

By September, however, Pym was a sick man, too ill to attend Commons, and the task of persuading Parliament to accept the agreement fell to St. John.[5] Contemporaries saw plainly St. John's emergence as a new parliamentary leader. Robert Baillie called him "that sweet man, Mr. Pym's successor." *Mercurius Britannicus* described him as the "one that hath lighted the candle of Mr. Pym's flames of zeal and piety, and now acts with so much virtue."[6]

Nevertheless, persuading Parliament to accept the Covenant was a prodigious task. The English and Scots retained their ancient distrust, and the Scots' determination to found a Presbyterian Church in England was regarded with apprehension by many MPs. Still, St. John labored doggedly in the fall of 1643 to convince Parliament of the virtues of aligning with the Scots. On 10 September, St. John urged members to lay aside religious differences for the good of the cause, and on 6 October he contended that an alliance with the Scots was vital to the success of the parliamentary cause.[7] The inclusion of the Scots would tip the military balance in Parliament's favor, he argued, and military superiority was the only way a meaningful and lasting settlement could be achieved.

The coming of the Scots aroused a deep and abiding resentment. St. John and Vane had agreed to the inclusion of a clause describing the Church of Scotland as "reformed according to the word of God." Many MPs were shocked by the idea that the Scots' concept of Church government was to be conceived as being reformed according to God's word.[8] The exact impact of the specter of Scottish Presbyterianism is difficult to gauge, but, clearly, the religious differences between the two kingdoms made cooperation difficult. The Covenant eventually was passed on 25 September 1643, but many MPs remained suspicious of the Scots and their Presbyterian system, distrusting them as deeply as they distrusted the King.[9]

One of the many opponents of the Solemn League and Covenant was Denzil Holles, leader of the peace party and most forceful advocate of a swift settlement with the King. Holles's response to the Covenant was to support the Lords' renewed call for peace negotiations in the hope that a settlement would alleviate the need for the Scots' presence in the war.[10] Before the outbreak of the civil war, Holles had been a leading critic of royal policy, and he was one of the Five Members whom Charles tried to arrest in January 1642. But the outbreak of the civil war had a sobering effect on him, and he began advocating coming to terms with the King as rapidly as possible.[11]

Holles's advocacy of a peace policy clashed with the more aggressive stance that St. John appeared to be pursuing. There was already bad blood between the two men. Whereas, in the spring of 1641, St. John had made a bitter speech against Strafford, had advocated a financial settlement with the King, and had written the Root and Branch Bill, Holles had worked to save his relative Strafford, had blocked St. John's fiscal reforms, and had not been as bitterly opposed as St. John to episcopacy.[12]

Moreover, St. John's militant noises in defense of the Covenant suggest that he had already begun to part company with the earl of Essex, Parliament's foremost general. Essex had been a cornerstone of Pym's policy. When war broke out in 1642, parliamentary leaders faced a basic problem in military organization. They needed to create an army free from the control of the localists, who cared only for limited, local goals and little for long-range, strategic aims.[13] They also needed to satisfy those who wanted the war against the King to be as limited as possible in order to facilitate a swift settlement, as opposed to those who wanted total war and a complete humbling of the King. At the beginning of the war, Essex was the only man who could possibly satisfy both groups. His military experience heartened the more militant members; his fundamental conservatism reassured the more moderate ones.[14]

Essex proved instead to be an inept commander, and his lack of aggressiveness infuriated the war party. For nearly a year after Edgehill, he failed to engage the King in a major battle. Cries against Essex sounded in Commons. Henry Marten attacked him openly, and Thomas Hoyle expressed fears that Essex's slowness would ruin the kingdom.[15] In the summer of 1643, Parliament's military fortunes were in a desultory state, and St. John's enthusiasm apparently dimmed. His speech for the Solemn League and Covenant on 6 October, advocating aggressive pursuance of the war, suggests his dissatisfaction with Essex's strategy. Moreover, the inclusion of the Scots would necessarily curb Essex's authority.

Hostility between St. John and Essex erupted in the debates over the treachery of Henry Rich, earl of Holland. During the summer of 1643, Holland tried to persuade Essex, his close friend, to support a peace program amounting to abject capitulation to the King. Essex refused. Coldly received by the Royalists, however, Holland switched sides again, and Essex encouraged him to return to Parliament. In November 1643, without remorse or apology, Holland returned to his seat in the House of Lords. The peers greeted him with affection;

the Commons did not. John Gurdon, a consistent and convinced war party man, announced that he preferred to pardon all the Lords at Oxford rather than this one.[16] Shortly after, St. John's right-hand man, Samuel Browne, suggested that Holland should be impeached for high treason.[17]

The division that followed revealed a telling sign that the middle way of Pym was eroding. War party men—such as Strode, Haselrig, and Gurdon—predictably supported Browne's proposal, while peace party men—such as Holles, Maynard, and Rudyard—just as predictably opposed it. But a split occurred among MPs who had previously aligned with Pym. St. John joined with Vane and the war party to vote against the proposal, whereas Sir Philip Stapleton, presumbly supporting Holles, acted as a teller against it.[18]

Essex, outraged at the charges against Holland, countered that St. John and Vane should be impeached instead.[19] This move seems curious. Why should Essex accuse St. John, his presumed ally in the middle party, and not Browne, Holland's actual accuser? The answer may be that the connection between St. John and Essex was tenuous at best, and that Essex already had reason to believe that St. John was his real enemy and Browne was merely a hatchet man. Two weeks earlier, St. John had joined with the radicals Arthur Haselrig and Peter Wentworth to demand that Essex issue a more liberal commission to his rival for command, Sir William Waller. St. John also proposed a full examination of all commissions previously issued.[20] Although St. John voiced no criticism of Essex, in view of the course of the war to that point, such an investigation had every chance of implicating Essex. Thus, by January 1644, Essex had good reason to be suspicious of St. John, whose speeches on the Solemn League and Covenant, apparent preference for Waller, and visible animosity toward Holland suggested that he was no friend of Essex and might have been trying to undermine him.

These disputes provide the background for the establishment of the Committee of Both Kingdoms, which was to facilitate cooperation with the Scots. Instead, it further diluted the power of Essex by dividing authority among Essex, the Scots, and members of Parliament. The hardening of opinion also was apparent. After an initial rejection of the bill to establish the committee, former middle groupers St. John, Sir Thomas Barrington, and John Crewe joined with Vane and Marten of the war party. Holles, Stapleton, and Glynn, also former middle groupers, opposed it. Essex, realizing that the proposal meant a further reduction in his power, made a frantic, but futile, effort to quash the bill in the House of Lords.[21]

It is true that St. John never committed himself publicly on the

Essex question. Indeed, Clarendon considered St. John to be one of Essex's supporters until debates on the Self-Denying Ordinance.[22] Such reticence is no doubt the mark of a prudent man. St. John's views on the Church question are similarly elusive.[23] In the case of Essex, however, the proposals he supported reveal his true feelings. Almost every move advanced or supported by St. John while leader of the Commons was damaging or potentially damaging to Essex. St. John's actions were part of a major upheaval that seems to have transformed parliamentary politics in 1643 and 1644. The Covenant with the Scots injected yet another religious dimension into politics. The death of Pym provided a leadership opportunity for those less committed to moderate goals. The dispute over Holland sharpened personal rivalries. The military failure of Essex created hostility toward aristocractic commanders. The "party" led by St. John did not necessarily sweep all before it or become a party in the modern sense, but the middle way of Pym was seriously disturbed, if not discarded. Whereas Pym had made every effort to accommodate dissident groups, St. John's policy seems to have been the reverse. His inclination was to cooperate almost entirely with the war party.

Military quarrels increased in intensity in the summer of 1644 as some new disputants appeared. Spurred by Oliver Cromwell, the parliamentary army and the Scots defeated Rupert and the royal army at Marston Moor on 2 July 1644. Shortly after the victory, arguments over strategy were revived. The commander of the Army of the Eastern Association, the earl of Manchester, seemingly lost his will to fight. He seemed loath to make decisions and reluctant to press the advantage gained at Marston Moor. Cromwell, on the other hand, proposed engaging the king as quickly as possible to secure a decisive victory. A bitter and acrimonious debate between the two men followed.

At the heart of the matter lay the same dilemma that had divided Parliament since the outbreak of the war. Manchester feared that the victory at Marston Moor suggested a decisive Roundhead victory, a triumph that could conceivably place England on the abyss of anarchy. In this fear Manchester was not alone. As D'Ewes lamented, "all right and property must cease in a civil war . . . and we know not what advantage the meaner sort may take to divide the spoils of the rich and noble among them."[24] Like many conservative Parliamentarians, Manchester and D'Ewes feared that the king's defeat would mean social anarchy and might eliminate essential hierarchical distinctions. As Denzil Holles expressed it, "the wisest of men saw it to be a great evil that servants should ride on horses."[25] Essex concurred, saying, "Our posterity will say that to deliver them from the yoke of the King, we have subjected them to the yoke of the common people."[26]

Admission of common folk into the war was the matter disputed by Manchester and Cromwell. When Cromwell angrily accused Manchester of holding back to avoid defeating the king, Manchester retaliated by charging Cromwell with courting the basest elements in society by sweeping away "honest gentlemen" and replacing them with "common men, poor and of mean parentage." Under Cromwell's guidance, one of his opponents complained, the Isle of Ely had become a "mere Amsterdam," with soldiers preaching from church pulpits that ordinary ministers dared not enter.[27]

Despite Manchester's charges, Cromwell entertained not the slightest idea of reconstructing society. He was, however, determined to defeat the King and willing to promote godly men, who happened to be sectaries, in quest of his goal. By all signs, Oliver St. John concurred with Cromwell, and his principal task in the fall of 1644 was maintaining his ties with Cromwell without alienating the Scots. This maneuver required delicacy. The Scots and Cromwell seemed mutually exclusive. The Scots disliked Cromwell for his hostility toward Presbyterianism and for ignoring their contribution to the victory at Marston Moor. They were dismayed, then, when their presumed ally, St. John, supported by Vane and Cromwell, publicly stated his preference for toleration of the sects.[28] Robert Baillie, the Scottish correspondent, claimed that St. John had "betrayed" the Scots. Baillie was so distressed that he even began to extol the virtues of the earl of Essex, whom he had previously considered incompetent, as military commander.[29]

In the face of this seeming treachery, the Scots temporarily abandoned St. John and Vane. On 10 November 1644 the French agent Sabran reported that the Scots had gone over to the peace party.[30] By December the Scots displayed visible opposition to the war party. They supported Manchester in his quarrel with Cromwell, accusing Cromwell of trying to drive a wedge between the nations of England and Scotland. And they convened at the earl of Essex's house to devise ways of subverting Cromwell.[31]

St. John and Vane, however, could not yet afford to scorn the Scots completely. Parliament's military prospects remained dreary in the fall of 1644. Marston Moor had been a great victory, but it had required the Scots' assistance. Moreover, Essex had been forced to surrender his army at Lostwithiel; the second battle at Newbury was indecisive; and the king's forces had relieved the siege at Donnington Castle.

"The harvest is past, the summer is ended, and we are not saved," mourned Thomas Hill.[32] Even Cromwell worried that his men were so exhausted that no further effort could be expected of them.[33]

Faced with the problem of Scottish defection and the burden of stodgy aristocratic command, St. John and Vane apparently contrived a solution for both problems. On 9 December 1644 the Presbyterian war party man Zouch Tate proposed an ordinance for self-denial by which all members of Parliament would resign their military commands. In one stroke the problems of command and the Scots could be solved. The war party could purge aristocratic commanders. The Scots, too, would be pleased; Cromwell would have to sacrifice his command.[34] On 11 December, St. John pleaded for passage of the ordinance as the only way to win the war.[35] Cromwell, with seeming magnanimity, agreed that it must be implemented, and it passed the Commons without a division on 19 December.[36]

The Scots were delighted. Both Robert Baillie and the *Scottish Dove*, the news sheet most often representative of the Scots' position, hailed the ordinance as a mighty step toward Parliament's deliverance. As the *Dove* noted, "in this vote more differences are resolved at one time than a whole year could have ended."[37]

St. John and Vane, of course, were not finished. In January 1645 they proposed the creation of a new national army under direct parliamentary supervision. Known as the New Model Army, the new force was designed to consist of 21,000 men to be paid from assessments. The salient feature of the New Model Army was that it centralized Parliament's entire military operation. Combined with the Self-Denying Ordinance, the New Model Army freed Parliament of the burden of divided and uncoordinated leadership.

In many respects the New Model Army was the product of consensus decision making.[38] Its composition, finance, and organization differed little from previous armies. Compromise had seemingly solved the problem of command. Sir Thomas Fairfax and Philip Skippon, the army's new commanders, were acceptable to both sides. Both possessed sound military reputations and were unsullied by previous quarrels. Neither man held extremist views in religion, other than a desire for godly reformation.

This development does not mean that army reform was universally applauded. Several elements, particularly in the Self-Denying Ordinance, aroused suspicion. First, members in the Commons could retain their commands by resigning their seats, an option not open to commanders in the Lords. Second, whereas Fairfax was specifically named commander-in-chief and Skippon major general of foot, the name of the major general of horse was mysteriously left blank.

Holles and other peace party men—such as Philip Stapleton, John Glynn, and Bulstrode Whitelocke—opposed both the Self-Denying Ordinance and the new modeling of the army. Whitelocke had no doubt that the ordinance for self-denial was aimed directly at Essex, because "he was too much a favorer of peace."[39] The ordinance also raised stern opposition among the Lords, who stood to lose two of their number, Manchester and Essex. In the end only the fear of a local riot convinced the Lords to pass the measure.[40]

Content with the apparent ruin of Cromwell, the Scots remained aloof from the debates on army reform. Despite their brief union with the peace party in December, the Scots made no effort to save Essex or to block the creation of the New Model. Satisfied with the ousting of Cromwell, the Scots simply observed the debates on army reform.[41]

The Scots had another reason for contentment. In January 1645 the fate of Archbishop Laud was being sealed. A despised symbol of "popish innovation," Laud had languished in the Tower since 1641. The furor aroused by Strafford's trial and execution probably saved Laud's life, at least temporarily, in the spring of 1641. Strafford's dignified but uncompromising defense won him many supporters, and—in the aftermath of the defections from the parliamentary ranks following Strafford's trial—Pym and the other parliamentary leaders may have decided that a treason trial involving Laud was too risky.[42]

Yet, in March 1644, proceedings against Laud began. Laud defended himself as resourcefully as Strafford had three years before, unwavering in his denial that he had ever assisted the Roman Church or had ever intended to "re-catholicize" England. Even Laud's chief prosecutor, William Prynne (also his victim in 1637), conceded that Laud's defense was "as full, as gallant . . . as was possible for the wit of man to invent."[43] At some point in the proceedings the prosecutors realized that Laud would almost certainly be acquitted on a treason charge, so they demanded that his guilt be determined by a bill of attainder. By this device Laud could be convicted by a simple majority vote in both houses, and Parliament had successfully employed this tactic against Strafford in 1641. From mid-November 1644 to January 1645, St. John and Vane repeatedly urged that the Lords adopt this course of action. On 4 January 1645 the Lords acquiesced. On 10 January, Laud was executed. "I have always lived in the Protestant religion as established in England, and in that I have come to die," he declared before laying his head on the block.[44]

Why were the proceedings against Laud revived after a three-year interval? Contemporaries were certain that Laud's execution had been contrived by St. John and Vane for the Scots' benefit. Sabran stated bluntly that "Laud was condemned to death for the Scots' benefit."

Mercurius Aulicus believed that Laud was executed because "things in Scotland could never remain the same if Canterbury remained alive." *Aulicus* also saw whom to blame. "The rebels have murdered the most reverend father in God, William Laud . . . Mr. St. John, Mr. Strode, Harbottle Grimston, and a few others undertake to dispatch him."[45]

If St. John revived the proceedings against Laud for the Scots' benefit, he had another compelling reason for doing so beyond army reform. The coming peace talks at Uxbridge made it imperative for St. John to keep the Scots in line. Disturbing signs had appeared that dissension existed in the Scots' ranks. On 30 January, Sabran reported that the Scots' Chancellor Loudon was willing to support the monarchy if Charles would abolish episcopacy.[46] As Parliament finished framing its proposals for the Uxbridge talks, several members were disturbed by the Scots' insistence that the religious question be settled before other matters were considered. This insistence aroused fears that the Scots—on persuading Charles to destroy episcopacy—would accede to him on other matters, such as the critical issue of militia control.[47]

In January 1645, then, St. John and Vane had good reason for courting the Scots. Army reform was critical in their eyes. Moreover, the temporary union of the peace party and the Scots in December suggested the possibility that the Scots, Holles, and the King might somehow manage to realize their common interests and reach a settlement. Understood in light of factional politics in 1644–45, St. John's behavior at Uxbridge becomes explicable. Clarendon reported that St. John and Vane acted as little more than watchdogs against Holles and the Royalists, displaying no inclination toward serious negotiation.[48] As it turned out, of course, Charles had no intention of compromising on religion, and the Uxbridge talks ended in failure. In January 1645, however, St. John could not have foreseen this result. He needed to take firm measures to block any possible alliance between the Scots and the Crown.

The insincerity of the temporary pro-Scottish policy employed by St. John and Vane became evident later in 1645. In April a second Self-Denying Ordinance was passed, exempting Cromwell. In August, with the mettle of the New Model Army proven by Cromwell's victory at Naseby in June, St. John and Vane abandoned the Scots. When Parliament considered measures for the establishment of a Presbyterian Church structure, St. John and Vane opposed them.[49]

Understood in terms of the factional struggles surrounding army reform, the timing of Laud's execution, too, becomes more understandable. In January 1645, St. John and Vane were striving to reform the army without alienating the Scots. Their campaign for Laud's execution and the Self-Denying Ordinance allowed them to reform the army without arousing Scottish suspicions that they might be eventually eased out, and at the same time prevented the Scots from defecting to the king or to Holles before the Uxbridge peace talks.

It would appear, therefore, that St. John had at last emerged as the leader he displayed the promise of becoming as early as the spring of 1641. The deaths of Pym and Hampden thrust him into the forefront of politics. St. John responded by undertaking a series of delicate maneuvers to take command of the army out of the hands of aristocratic commanders, and he succeeded in guiding the passage of legislation that created a more effective fighting force without, initially, driving away the Scots. It does not seem an exaggeration to suggest that, in 1645, St. John's parliamentary leadership was as critical to the parliamentary cause as Cromwell's military leadership. It is also interesting to note that St. John retained many of the political skills he had acquired in 1641. The man who induced others to introduce legislation he favored or authored—such as the Root and Branch or the Militia Bills—managed to dislodge Essex and, along with Vane, restructure the Army, without appearing until the latest stages to be the agent of that undertaking. St. John seems to have learned a lesson from his first experiences in parliamentary politics. After his initial fiery speeches on Ship Money and Strafford, St. John clearly changed his tactics, rarely making public pronouncements on the weightier matters of State, and remaining behind the scenes as much as possible.

6

Against the Current: St. John and Holles's Ascendancy

St. John's activities from the fall of 1643 through the summer of 1645 represent the zenith of his political power and influence. As we have seen, he and Vane purged the Army of some of its more dilatory commanders and installed the fighting force that ultimately won the war for Parliament. These triumphs required a political mastery comparable to that once displayed by Pym. St. John and Vane reduced the power and role of the Scots substantially without alienating them from the parliamentary cause.

This was a delicate path to follow, and there were indications that the Scots were beginning to become disenchanted with the party of St. John and Vane. Robert Baillie concluded as early as September 1644 that the Scots "must seek new friends at last when our old friends, without the least cause, have deserted us."[1] In early 1645, *Mercurius Aulicus* related that the Scottish Commissioners have "withdrawn their intimateness with those of the Committee of Both Kingdoms . . . and have joined themselves in conspiracy and compliance with Sir Philip Stapleton and his associates."[2] The defection of the Scots to Holles, however, was not yet complete. Holles and Stapleton had opposed the Solemn League and Covenant, and their alliance with the Scots—resting as it did on premises as weak and illusory as those on which St. John and Vane had courted them in 1643—would not be finalized until 1646. "Most of the House of Commons are downright Erastian," wrote Robert Baillie in 1645. "They are like to create us more woe than all the sectaries of England."[3]

While distancing himself from the Scots without yet rejecting them, St. John could also claim modest success in cementing relations between Parliament and the City of London, and in the area of finance as well. To secure his control over the London Common Council, St. John, in January 1644, introduced an ordinance to disenfranchise members of the Council who had been questioned for malignancy or who had refused to take the Solemn League and Covenant. The Council that emerged from these reforms—as well as John Fowlke, its dominant figure—supported St. John's efforts to reform the army.[4]

St. John's attempts to exert more control in the City and on his shaky coalition in Parliament may have been helped by his discovery of the Brooke Plot. St. John intercepted a letter that contained an unauthorized peace proposal to the King and a plan by the lord mayor and several aldermen to proclaim the Oxford Parliament the only true Parliament. St. John claimed that he discovered this letter in the fireplace of a leading London papist, Sir Basil Brooke.[5] Even though the fireplace story appears too lurid to be creditable, the idea that leading City authorities could be dealing secretly with the King was disturbing, and, on St. John's motion, the Brooke Plot was condemned by the Commons. Seeking reconciliation, City officials organized a banquet for the Scots, leading figures in parliament, and the Assembly of Divines. On the same day Stephen Marshall inveighed mightily against "those insidious forces who divide the City from Parliament, each house from the other, and the English from the Scots." Marshall concluded with an appeal to all parties committed to the parliamentary cause, asserting to them that it was essential to remain vigilant and united against royal plotting. There is no evidence to prove it, but the Brooke Plot looks like an episode exploited by St. John to maintain the unity of his own fragile coalition.[6]

In matters of finance St. John and Vane sought to avoid imposing further tax burdens by granting monopolies to powerful companies in return for loans. The Merchant Adventurers, for example, loaned Parliament £40,000 between October 1643 and January 1644 in return for trading concessions more favorable than those they had enjoyed under Charles. On 24 January 1644, Parliament borrowed another £6,000 from the East India Company, and, on 29 January, Parliament secured an additional £8,000 from the Levant Company. Securing this series of loans, however, did not guarantee financial security or solvency. Expecting a short war, Parliament had elected initially to offer high pay for soldiers and officers, and it had failed to implement an adequate fiscal operation. Parliament's failure to achieve a quick victory in the field, and its need for more men, only compounded its financial problems. On 4 March 1644, St. John and Vane advanced a new plan, combining loans from businesses and mortgages of real estate. They expected a yield of £200,000, and they offered the lands of delinquents, Catholics, and bishops as security.[7] Although these measures failed to address Parliament's long-range financial problems, St. John—even if all his efforts did not succeed and his allegiances were not exactly rock solid—came dauntingly close to constructing a workable alliance between the various components of the parliamentary power structure.

St. John's increased political prominence also made him a target for attack. In June 1645, James Cranford, a well-known Presbyterian minister, circulated a report accusing St. John, Vane, Pierrepoint, and Crewe of appointing themselves—without authorization from Parliament—to serve as a subcommittee of the Committee of Both Kingdoms, and of conducting secret negotiations with the King.[8] Cranford's report alleged further that during the course of these negotiations St. John and the others offered to surrender parliamentary forts and installations. Cranford's charges were based on intelligence that he claimed had been provided to him by Baillie, who, according to Cranford, had informed him that Lord Digby had intercepted a letter containing peace propositions for the King. Baillie, however, claimed that he did not name particular MPs in his conversations with Cranford. In the contentious atmosphere of the summer of 1645, it is certainly possible that Cranford, a Presbyterian minister, perceived Baillie's information as a way to discredit supporters of toleration.[9]

Responding immediately to Cranford's charges, St. John admitted that a subcommittee of the Committee of Both Kingdoms existed, but that its purpose was to discover who was sending information to the King, and he claimed that the committee had been instructed to negotiate only about Royalist forts.[10] A parliamentary committee was then formed to investigate Cranford's charges, and, after a brief debate in early July, the Commons dismissed Cranford's charges and exonerated St. John. Cranford was sent to the Tower and ordered to pay £500 to each of the men whose reputations he had impugned.[11]

It is possible that St. John was engaged in secret negotiations with the King, but it is not likely that he was prepared to surrender parliamentary garrisons. St. John's entire policy since 1643 had been designed to maneuver Parliament in such a way that it could negotiate from a position of military superiority. There is, however, another perplexity about the subcommittee exposed by Cranford that sheds additional light on St. John's attitude towards the treatment of the Scots after 1644. The subcommittee's formation was not recorded in the daybook of Parliament's activities. The Scots were not informed of its creation until a month after its establishment and the Scots' representative on the committee was never summoned to a meeting. Even Pierrepoint, whom St. John named as a member, declared that he was unaware of the committee's existence.[12]

The Cranford Affair was only a prelude to a larger political struggle in the summer of 1645. Throughout the spring and summer of 1645, the already tangled web of parliamentary politics was further confused by another series of intrigues, clandestine meetings, and charges of secret negotiations between moderate parliamentarians and the Scots. The moderates, most visibly Holles, appear to have been in contact with the royal headquarters at Oxford during this time. The unscrupulous and dissembling Lord Savile played a leading part in these negotiations. A critic of government policy in 1640, Savile was a Royalist in 1645. Mistrusted by both sides, Savile had retired to France in early 1645. Hearing of the possibility that the Uxbridge peace talks might be reopened, Savile suddenly returned to England and quickly became involved in an intricate round of plots, again kindling charges and countercharges on both sides.[13]

Savile's first audience was with the Scottish Chancellor Loudon, and by mid-May he had managed an exchange with St. John and Say. Savile believed that there were signs that war party members were willing to retreat from the uncompromising stance they had taken at Uxbridge. For the first time they were willing to share control of the militia with the king, allowing Charles to name one-fourth to one-third of the commissioners.[14] Holles later claimed that Savile's maneuverings cloaked a secret bargain in which St. John would become lord keeper.[15] Savile also seems to have convinced St. John and Say that the war might be ended through the defection of the Royalist general George Goring and the governor of Oxford, William Legge. The failure of the Uxbridge negotations, claimed Savile, had created a general depression among Royalists, many of whom, he said, believed that the King should have been more willing to make concessions to Parliament.[16]

Savile's reputation was questionable, but St. John considered the matter serious enough to have a subcommittee of the Committee of Both Kingdoms investigate it. Shortly after the committee began its deliberations, St. John found himself under attack by Holles, who accused St. John, the earl of Northumberland, Saye, and Vane of "underhand dealings." St. John and Vane replied with countercharges of Holles's complicity with Oxford.[17] Savile then informed the subcommittee that the Royalists had been provided with constant reports of the proceedings in the Commons by Holles. Furious, Holles denounced the charge as totally false. When Bulstrode Whitelocke, a member of the committee, reported to the Commons that Savile had refused to divulge the source of his information about Holles, Savile was ordered to the Tower.[18]

Cromwell's dramatic victory at Naseby in June 1645 may have convinced war party men to take bolder measures against Holles. On

2 July, John Gurdon reported to the Commons that Savile had accused Holles and Whitelocke of treason at the Uxbridge negotiations.
Holles, according to Savile, had promised the King that he would
persuade the Commons "to yield to such proposals as the King
should make." Moreover, Holles allegedly assured the King that the
Scots were weary of dealing with the "violent spirits" and were willing
to seek new allies.[19]

Under close examination Holles admitted that he had discussed
peace proposals with Royalist emissaries, but he denied any disloyalty
to Parliament. His admission of contact, however, was enough to fuel
more suspicions of duplicity, and John Gurdon demanded that Holles
be sent to the Tower. A new committee was formed to consider the
charges and was chaired by St. John's cousin and close friend Samuel
Browne.[20] Quickly, Holles's friends began laboring diligently on his
behalf. One of them, Lambert Osbaldeston, went directly to St. John
to persuade him to drop the charges, indicating that, despite the
appointment of Browne to chair the committee, contemporaries still
perceived that St. John was the real power behind the scene.[21] Osbaldeston returned from the meeting convinced that St. John and his
associates were "resolved to ruin Holles if they could."[22]

Holles was rescued by the intervention of the Scots. They came
forward with three notes, written in Savile's hand, containing conclusive evidence of Savile's Royalist sympathies. The possibility that
Savile was a closet Royalist cast further doubt on his already questionable credibility. Although Holles was not completely exonerated, the
charges against him were dropped.[23]

The Savile Affair had far reaching implications for both Holles and
St. John. Holles was temporarily discredited, but in the long run the
attempt to ruin him backfired. The charges against Holles were so
vague, and Savile so obviously unreliable, that St. John and Vane
appeared to be partners in a partisan and contrived vendetta against
Holles.[24] As well, the Scots, once closely aligned with St. John and
openly hostile to Holles, transmitted another signal that their connection with St. John was becoming increasingly tenuous.

In 1645 contemporaries began to apply the terms "Presbyterian"
and "Independent" to distinguish between the political groups in the
Long Parliament. Clarendon believed that these terms began to be
used in March 1645 after the failure of the Uxbridge negotiations.[25]
In Clarendon's mind the label "Presbyterian" could be applied to
those members who were most interested in settling with the King,
opposed toleration, and supported a moderate Presbytery, free of
parliamentary control, to maintain discipline. By contrast, for Clarendon, the Independents consisted of those members who demanded

a rigorous settlement with the King, depriving Charles of many of his prerogative powers, while advocating religious toleration and parliamentary control over any Church settlement.

Historians have become suspicious of the assessments of contemporary observers like Baillie and Clarendon who perceived the Presbyterians and Independents to be mutually exclusive groups locked in mortal combat against each other.[26] Denzil Holles himself, for example, leader of the Presbyterian Party, as identified by most contemporaries, was by no means a religious Presbyterian; his most recent biographer believes that he was an Erastian.[27] Holles's closest subordinate, Sir Philip Stapleton, was said to devote more time to his dogs, horses, and soldiering than to religious observances. On the other hand, Sir Henry Vane the Younger, usually classed as an Independent, helped negotiate the entry of the Presbyterian Scots into the war on Parliament's side and—along with other political Independents, such as Edmund Prideaux—was identified by D'Ewes as promoting "ultra Presbyterian" legislation. Finally, Zouch Tate, the staunch war party man, who had introduced the ordinance for the New Model Army, was an equally staunch religious Presbyterian. Thus, it was clearly possible for a member to be a religious Presbyterian and support Independent political policies, and equally possible, in the case of Holles, to be an Erastian while supporting Presbyterian political ideas.

Oliver St. John, who has commonly been classed as a typical political Independent, serves as a good example of the inefficacy of the Presbyterian/Independent labels. St. John's views on the Constitution, law and order were perfectly compatible with those of Holles and other political Presbyterians. Although St. John preferred a sterner settlement with the King than Holles favored, Holles was not prepared to make an easy capitulation to the King, either, and St. John was also fairly close to Holles in religion. As Valerie Pearl demonstrated years ago, St. John was certainly not a religious Independent.[28] St. John's eclecticism in matters of religion is hard to doubt. His Calvinist sympathies emerge in his correspondence with Cromwell and in his personal commonplace book. His Erastianism is demonstrated through his support for religious toleration and his insistence on parliamentary control of ecclesiastical matters. Finally, in 1647, St. John helped install James Ussher, archbishop of Armagh and a supporter of a moderate episcopacy, as a preacher at Lincoln's Inn. St. John later joined Ussher's prayer circle, and the two become regular dinner companions.[29]

Although recent scholars examining civil war politics, almost without exception, have emphasized the shifting, transitory nature of the political groupings described here and the baffling contradictions and incongruities that often arose, it must be stressed again that none of the "parties" described here sustained a formal organization.[30] They were informal groupings, shifting and ephemeral. Nor can the basic structuring of party groups—St. John/Vane, Marten/Haselrig, Holles/Stapleton—be said to exhaust the possible groupings. Even the idea of party itself is a concept of limited value. Few MPs adhered consistently to a particular faction, and fewer still would have regarded themselves as "supporters" or "adherents" of one of the various groups.

Nevertheless, St. John, along with Vane, usually was perceived by comtemporaries as the head of a group, and one that often captured majority support. Religious Presbyterians—such as Tate, Prideaux, and Browne—usually voted with St. John, as did moderate Episcopalians—such as Crewe and Pierrepoint. Genuine radicals like Marten also supported St. John's policies on occasion, as did Haselrig. Temperamentally, St. John probably had the most in common with a true religious and political Independent, Nathaniel Fiennes. In his manifesto of Independency, *Vindiciae Veritatis,* Fiennes contended that the Independents "resolve therefore to keep the three estates coordinate equally to praise and blame each other. . . . We need not, we will not to gain a peace, be without a King, nor without this King: only he himself hath brought this necessity upon us, not to trust him with that power whereby he may do us and himself harm."[31] Unfortunately, we do not know what St. John thought about *Vindiciae Veritatis,* but the ideas expressed in it provide precise definition of and correspond to the position that St. John and those who most often voted with him appeared to support: settlement with the King through a realistic, resolute combination of war and negotiation to ensure that the political revolution of 1640–42 was not compromised and the security of those who initiated that revolution was not endangered.

The entire structure of politics, as well as political groupings, became even more confused and blurred after the end of the first civil war. In the fall of 1646 the Royalist war effort crumbled. In September parliamentary forces compelled Rupert to surrender Bristol, thereby enabling Parliament to secure control of the southwest. A few days later, the King's forces in Scotland, under the command of James Graham, the earl of Montrose, were defeated by the Covenanters at Philiphaugh. Faced with this series of debilitating defeats, Charles—after trying desperately to negotiate with the Irish or the French—surrendered to the Scots in April 1646.

Many members expected that, with the conclusion of four years of desultory conflict, a settlement with the King could be easily attained and the political deadlock broken. Victory, however, did not bring the anticipated satisfaction and resolution. In fact, the possibility of reaching a settlement became more remote. Charles's correspondence with the Irish had been intercepted, and even members who retained some sympathy for the king must have been shaken by revelations that Charles could still contemplate the use of Irish troops against Parliament. Moreover, his internment with the Scots raised fears that he might yet negotiate a deal with them by yielding to their insistence on Presbyterianism, revive the Royalist forces, and use a combined army to reopen the war. These fears, however, were based on the assumption that Charles understood the Scots' commitment to a Presbyterian Church and that he was willing to compromise his own religious principles. Retrospectively, it is possible to see that, in 1646, at least, neither of these assumptions was true. Charles was utterly unable to comprehend the religious convictions of the Scots, and he apparently believed that they would offer concessions to him.

The conclusion of the war also altered the balance of power in parliamentary politics. Since the fall of 1643, St. John and Vane had, despite occasional setbacks, artfully controlled Parliament. But, strengthened by the return of absentee members frightened off by the war and supported by new members who had won seats in "recruiter" elections, the party of Denzil Holles began to assume a position from which it could challenge St. John and Vane for leadership.[32]

St. John and Vane resisted at this point coming to terms with the King, and by the spring of 1646 there is evidence that their adherence to this policy was costing them votes. In April the King left Oxford in disguise and journeyed toward London, apparently expecting a joyous welcome. St. John and Vane refused to deal with him, and the Commons engaged in a debate over some intercepted correspondence between the King and his Scottish captors.[33] Alarmed, St. John and Vane undertook a late-night expedition to the rooms of the lord mayor of London, fearing that he intended to help the King. St. John's and Vane's sense of alarm increased when they discovered letters in the possession of the lord mayor that described them—along with Samuel Browne and Henry Marten—speaking during the Commons' discussion of the King's surrender to the Scots, "boldly with foul expressions."[34] St. John and Vane were singled out for having "shamefully traduced."[35] When St. John and Vane wished to explore the matter further in the Commons, their plans were rejected. Several days later, they were defeated again when they attempted to block any Scottish participation in peace proposals concerning England, and on 21 May they also failed to prevent a move to reopen debate on Church government.[36]

At this point St. John and Vane confronted a problem faced by many successful wartime leaders. The aggressive policies necessary to win a war become irrelevant and often resented in peacetime. During the course of 1646, Holles began to capture that moderate body of support, previously controlled by St. John and Vane, because his political ideas addressed the peacetime concerns of many members. As the year progressed, it became evident that Holles's policies had three main components. First, the New Model Army would be disbanded. Successful disbandment would reduce county resentment at the taxation necessary to sustain the war effort, eliminate men whom Holles suspected of radicalism, and deprive St. John and Vane of an essential ally. Second, Holles planned to allow several "trusted" regiments and commanders to remain in service to reconquer Ireland. Finally, Holles proposed to sell off the lands and possessions of the clergy to pay off English and Scottish troops and provide revenue for the war in Ireland.[37]

Holles's policies appealed powerfully to men who wished to reach a settlement with the King, who feared sectarian radicalism in the Army, and who sought a means to relieve the tax burdens imposed on the counties. The New Model Army and the war effort had imposed a greater tax burden on the localities than Charles ever had, and many members recognized that, even with the King defeated, they still had another revolutionary specter with which to contend—the discontented masses.

Skillfully presented, these policies also had the virtue, from Holles's point of view, of bringing the City and the Scots into a coalition with him against St. John and Vane. Moreover, Holles's proposals for the confiscation and sale of church lands and possessions gave the Scots hope not only that their form of Church government might be implemented but that they might actually be paid for their time in England. The City's flight, to Holles, was a more important reversal. As we have seen, St. John attempted to maintain close ties with the City leadership between 1643 and 1645. But, with the war won, the city's leaders feared the army's radicalism, and Holles's plans gave them their best hope for repayment of the loans they had made to continue the war effort.

Holles's strategy did contain some risks. Many members, not necessarily those connected with St. John and Vane, still doubted that Charles could be trusted to abide by any settlement. Other members questioned whether the Covenanters' contribution to the war effort merited the kind of settlement Holles desired. Holles was certainly no religious Presbyterian, but his belief that the Scottish Army should be generously compensated clashed with the traditional English distaste for the Covenanters. Furthermore Holles was still suspected—especially in the aftermath of the Savile Affair—of plotting a total capitulation to the King. During the war St. John and Vane had endeavored to maintain at least a surface unity, but, in late 1646, divisions were called as often as in the contentious days of 1641.[38]

In their assessments of the postwar political situation, St. John and Holles actually agreed on several key questions. Neither was a revolutionary, calling for a drastic overhaul of existing government. Both were Erastians, unwilling to support *jus divino* Presbyterianism or to confer limited power of discipline upon ecclesiastical authority. On 6 March 1646, Holles carried up to the House of Lords a religious bill, which he called the "dawning of a glorious day," and which contained provisions for lay commissioners to monitor the progress of religious reform.[39] The Scots were bitterly disappointed in the religious settlement proposed in the bill, which Baillie derided as a "lame Erastian Presbytery."[40] Moreover, neither St. John nor Holles was prepared to accept a political settlement that did not include the King. Holles labored endlessly to hammer out an agreement with the King, and Valerie Pearl long ago demonstrated St. John's similar concerns. Here, however, the similarities end and the real differences between the two surface. St. John supported religious toleration; Holles was an implacable opponent. Holles believed that the New Model Army was a dangerous sectarian force; St. John, as will be shown, was by no means committed unerringly to the Army, but he did recognize its importance to both Parliament's and his personal interests. Finally, Holles, a former fiery spirit who had become more circumspect, by 1646 had a history of moderate, pro-Charles activities. St. John, a man involved in Strafford's execution, the Militia Bill, and the creation of the New Model Army, had much more to fear from a Royalist victory and understandably demanded more rigorous safeguards in a settlement that Holles was prepared to concede.

Contemporary news sheets, however, cried for a settlement in the late summer and fall of 1646, and they occasionally displayed or observed surprising support for the King. The *Weekly Intelligencer* argued that there should be no diminution of His Majesty's powers and greatness. But a Republican pamphlet accused London politicians of a willingness to surrender to the King on any terms.[41] Hope for peace centered primarily on the Newcastle Propositions, which repeated many of the demands presented to the King at Uxbridge. Charles was asked to yield many of his executive powers. The Newcastle Propositions requested, among other things, parliamentary control of the militia for the next twenty years, severe punishments for papists and delinquents, and the disqualification of Royalists from future appointments.[42]

The Newcastle Propositions embodied a governance structure that appeared to be close to that which St. John had been advocating since the war's inception. We do not, however, know his role in the genesis of the Newcastle Propositions, although he later expressed qualified support for them in the fall of 1646.[43] However, there are slight, but recurring, indications that St. John's policies were coming under fire, and that he was losing some of the influence he had enjoyed since 1645. As early as March 1645, D'Ewes commented that "Mr. Sollicitor [sic], young Vane, Pierrepoint, and others moved to set out some new declaration for all men to come in upon as good terms as was proposed in the Articles of the late treaties, etc., but no vote was passed."[44]

St. John's prestige may also have suffered slightly from his association with Vane. Vane possessed enormous personal charm and political dexterity, but by 1646 he had also acquired a reputation for using power to serve his own interests. Particularly offensive to members was Vane's refusal to return half of the profits he obtained from serving as secretary of the navy. Thus, John Lilburne's charge that Vane and St. John were "covetous catchworms" had merit when applied to Vane. St. John was tarnished by the same brush, although later Holles also accused St. John of being motivated by personal aggrandizement.[45]

Reflecting on the events of early 1646, Lilburne also claimed to have "anatomzied the baseness" of St. John and Vane.[46] Here, Lilburne's bitterness went deeper than a mere crusade against corruption. In June 1646 he had been committed to the Tower by the House of Lords for his denunciation of the earl of Manchester's military record, and he expected that at any moment his friends in the Commons would rescue him. When the Commons failed to intercede, Lilburne began to urge reform of Parliament itself. His complete philosophy had not yet emerged, but, in a steady stream of pamphlets and broadsides, Lilburne demanded extension of the franchise and annual Parliaments, asserting repeatedly that the Commons derived its power from the people alone. In his view,

> Parliament tyrannizeth ten times more over us than the King did . . . and I will maintain that by the law of the Kingdom, it is ten times easier to prove it lawful for us to take up arms against them . . . than it was them to take up arms against the King . . . tyranny is . . . resistible in a Parliament as well as a King.[47]

Lilburne's alienation from the parliamentary cause may help us understand further the difficult path St. John walked in 1646. Lilburne's charge must have been particularly troubling. St. John was first and foremost a Parliament man. From his Ship Money days when he defended Parliament's historic right to approve direct taxation, St. John had repeatedly demonstrated his belief in the efficacy of Parliament. Now, parliamentary authority was being derided by a source that previously had been friendly.

Faced with challenges on several fronts in the summer of 1646, St. John continued to battle to retain his authority. The Newcastle Propositions offered renewed hope for a settlement with the King. But on 1 August 1646, Charles rejected the Newcastle Propositions on the grounds that they "imported such great alterations in government both in Church and Kingdom as it were very difficult to return a particular and a positive answer before a full debate. . . ."[48] On 13 August the two Houses of Parliament held a joint conference to consider the implications of the King's refusal. With their latest offer spurned, Parliament elected to redirect its energies toward settling with the Scots. Holles and Stapleton took the initiative in this undertaking, and by September they had persuaded the Commons to vote a total of £400,000. Initially, the Commons consented to an initial payment of £200,000 and a total of £400,000.[49] The Commons "deeply resented this," John Harington noted, but, after what Holles later recalled as a "strong" debate, it agreed to the terms.[50] On 5 September, Holles chaired a committee formed to approach the City about lending the money, and offering all former lenders the opportunity to double their original investment and obtain the bishops' lands in return. As Baillie observed, the Commons' action insured that the funds would be generated immediately, and that the bishops' lands would be confiscated "in a way that no skill would get them back again."[51]

Although they did not finally surrender the King to Parliament until February 1647, the Scots agreed to Parliament's terms because they found Charles as exasperating as Parliament had. Charles still failed to grasp the Covenanters' devotion to Presbyterianism and gave no indication that he would accept the kind of religious settlement the Scots desired. Their departure, however, vastly improved the position of the political Presbyterians in Parliament, because they no longer had to defend themselves from the charge that they were plotting to join up with the Scots. Their enhanced prestige was noted in one newsletter. "The Presbyterian Party," remarked one correspondent in December 1646, "now carry all votes. . . ."[52]

Even though his ability to influence Parliament had declined in 1646, St. John was not yet prepared to concede defeat. In fact, the removal of the Scots and their transfer of the King were policies that he could endorse. Without the Scots, the power of the New Model Army loomed larger, and St. John was astute enough to perceive that

Holles's next move would be to disband it. In September 1646, St. John introduced into the record comments from French observers advising Parliament "not to disband the army of Fairfax, that all hereby would be lost."[53] On 7 October, Holles's supporters failed to even contest an order to extend the army's life for another six months.

At the same time he was fighting to preserve the Army's existence, St. John tended to another matter in October 1646. Perhaps irritated at the King's rejection of the peace proposals, St. John on 4 October advanced the argument that the Newcastle Propositions should be converted into parliamentary ordinances and become law whether the king signed them or not.[55] A few days later, on 21 October, St. John, Haselrig, and Mildmay pressed for a bizarre scheme "for regulating both houses of Parliament and their committees."[56]

Precisely what St. John had in mind is not immediately evident, but one alarmed member responded by declaring that "having won the kingdom by the sword they can dispose of it as a just conquest." This member apparently believed that St. John was dropping a thinly veiled hint to turn the New Model Army against his opponents in Parliament.[57] Thus, it was not completely without reason that Montreuil refused to concede Holles's dominance.[58]

As 1646 came to a close, confusion pervaded among the competing groups at Westminster. On the one hand, primarily upon Holles's initiative, a religious settlement had been reached; the Scots had been paid off; and in the Newcastle Propositions a serious overture to the King had been undertaken. On the other hand, Charles had been defeated in February; it was now December, and settlement remained leagues away.

Neither of the principal factions at Parliament, those of Holles or of St. John, had been able to acquire complete dominance, although Holles had cut some serious inroads into St. John's influence. Curiously, while there was distrust and personal animosity on both sides from the Savile Affair, the two parties were not irreparably divided.[59] Neither was irrevocably opposed to a settlement, and several difficult issues had been resolved. Erastians on both sides desired parliamentary control of a state church with limited powers of discipline; the Newcastle Propositions provided at least a starting point for future negotiations with the King; and a majority in Parliament were not yet disposed to disband the New Model Army. Charles apparently believed that delay and procrastination would further divide supporters of both Holles and St. John, thus leading to a settlement more generous than that offered in the Newcastle Propositions, and he was probably correct. Whether destroying the fragile balance of power between the parliamentary factions was ultimately in the King's best interest, however, was another question.

7

Decline and Disillusion

"The Presbyterians," remarked one of the earl of Clarendon's correspondents in the spring of 1647, "now carry things with a high hand."[1] Holles had captured control because his scheme to disband the Army reflected both parliamentary and country hostility toward military rule. "We will destroy them all," declared the Presbyterian William Strode, ". . . Sir Thomas Fairfax will be deceived, for part of his army will join us, and besides the Scots are very honest men. . . ."[2] In the counties fears of renewed taxation and rumors of unruly soldiers frightening citizens all contributed to the atmosphere that allowed Holles to take charge.

In his *Memoirs,* Holles depicted a titanic struggle between his party and that of St. John, and he excoriated his opponents with page after page of vituperative invective. Haselrig, Vane, and Fairfax were condemned in uncompromising terms as "those visible saints," "children of darkness," and "implacable spirits." But Holles reserved his greatest scorn for Cromwell and St. John, "the two grand designers of the ruin of the three kingdoms."[3] Of the two, Holles considered St. John to be more dangerous because of his legal training and expertise. Holles contended that St. John's true and fatally flawed character was revealed when St. John abandoned his legal principles to secure Strafford's execution. In this "villainy" that could neither be "forgotten nor forgiven," St. John, according to Holles, destroyed the integrity of the cause they all originally sought to defend.[4]

Not surprisingly, Holles then blasted St. John for his role in the Savile Affair. But Holles's arguments in the *Memoirs* are nonetheless curious. St. John's prominence in Holles's assault is, on one level, understandable. From the time of the Strafford case through the military quarrels with Essex through the Savile Affair, St. John and Holles had clashed regularly. Yet, on another level the depth of animosity in Holles's attack on St. John is surprising. As we have seen, St. John and Holles had much in common. Whereas historians have often juxtaposed St. John the radical with Holles the moderate, it is clear that the men shared Erastian ideas, a distaste for anarchy, and a reluctance to restore the monarchy without adequate constitutional safeguards. St. John's desire for a settlement containing appropriate constitutional limits on the monarchy should be clear by this point. And William Lenthall was probably referring to Holles when he remarked, "I knew the Presbyterians would never restore the king to his just rights."[5]

On February 1647 the Commons voted to disband the New Model Army, leaving only 5,000 cavalry.[6] The question of Ireland remained, and, in March, Holles attempted to negotiate with the Army to engage soldiers for the Irish service. The soldiers, however, presented Sir Thomas Fairfax with a petition describing their resentment at not being paid for their service. Led by Holles, Parliament responded on 30 March with a declaration threatening to charge the soldiers as "enemies of the state" and stating their "high dislike of that petition."[7]

Whereas many regiments outside the New Model Army were demobilized without difficulty, the men of the New Model Army reacted angrily to the order to disband. In addition to its denunciation of the Army, Holles's declaration of 30 March also denied the soldiers the right to petition. After refusing to disperse, each regiment chose its own "Agitators" to represent them. Their first demand was full arrears of pay. When Holles tried to ignore them, they repaired to New Market and set up an Army council, consisting of the generals, plus two officers and two men from each regiment, to issue a statement of discontent.

Historians have labored mightily to understand the aims and ideology of the New Model Army. Traditionally, the Army's rank and file have been described as sectarian fanatics, "Saints in Arms," determined to reform Church and State along egalitarian lines. Recent research, however, has cast doubt on the belief that a majority of the troops were religious radicals or that egalitarian ideas were present at the Army's inception.[8] What does seem likely is that the New Model Army emerged from the first civil war with a sublime Calvinistic confidence that its victories were a sign of God's favor and with the conviction that the nation's destiny was in its hands. Holles's decision to disband the Army fueled suspicion in the ranks that he was determined to circumvent the Army's mission as England's deliverer and that Parliament as a whole was not in sympathy with the Army's messianic goals.

Holles did not intend to disband the army without pay. On 2 April the Commons formed a committee to arrange a £200,000 loan from the City of London. A month of intense negotiations followed, and in May the loan was finally secured. Despite all the difficulty with the loan, Holles still managed to raise only £200,000 of the £3,000,000 needed to meet the soldiers' arrears.[9]

The bottom soon fell out of Holles's plan. On 25 May 1647 the Commons voted again to disband the Army, beginning with Fairfax's regiment. On 1 June 1647, Fairfax replied with a letter expressing the Army's adamant refusal to disband. To further complicate Holles's plans, on 3 June, Cornet George Joyce, leading a troop of cavalry and fearing a conservative countermove against the Army, seized the King from parliamentary custody at Holmby House and remanded him to the Army's custody at Newmarket. Holles made a desperate attempt to reassure the Army of his good intentions towards them. But at the same time Holles was also striving to maintain the City's loyalty and urging it to stand firm against the Army if necessary. Holles, however, soon discovered that the City's resolve to resist the Army was weakening, and he blamed the Army, which, he asserted, "betwitched" City leaders and "lulled" them into a false sense of security.[10]

Events now rushed completely out of Holles's control. On 14 June the Army demanded the impeachment of Holles, Stapleton, and nine of their supporters, accusing them of raising "suspicions" against the Army, disbanding the Army in order to advance themselves, and attempting to raise new forces against the Army.[11] On 25 June, with the news that the Army was marching from St. Albans to Uxbridge, Holles requested permission for himself and the other accused members to withdraw from the house. With Holles and the City intimidated, the Army halted its march and withdrew to Richmond. In mid-July the eleven members returned to Parliament to defend themselves, but they abandoned the struggle on 20 July. On 22 July, following the Commons' vote to restore the London militia to Independent control, an unruly crowd of apprentices forced its way into Parliament, demanding that the Militia Ordinance be repealed and that the king be invited back to London. With this explosion of mob violence, counterrevolution appeared to be at hand. The next day, Ludlow, Haselrig, and several other Independent leaders decided to secede from Parliament and seek the Army's protection.[12] On 30 July, in the absence of the Independent leaders, the Presbyterians voted to return the eleven members and ordered the Army to remain at least thirty miles outside of London.[13]

Army leaders perceived these actions as preparations for a counterstroke. For Holles, everything depended on convincing the City to confront the Army. But once again, City politicians faltered, refusing to resist the Army or to protect the eleven members. When the triumphant Army entered London on 6 August, Holles and the other ten members fled.[14]

In slightly less than two months, Holles's six-month ascendancy had crumbled. Holles had primarily his own poor judgment to blame for his failure to retain power in the summer of 1647. Counting on the

City for support twice in the same summer was imprudent enough, and surely any student of Roman history—as most of the participants in the civil war were by education—must have understood the utter folly of trying to disband an unpaid, aroused, and sullen fighting force. From Sulla and Marius to Caesar and Octavian, the lesson of the Republic remained: whoever controlled the Army controlled Rome.

Despite the venom that Holles reserved for St. John in his *Memoirs,* St. John not only offered little resistance to the disbanding of the Army in the spring of 1647, but had little to do with the Army's return that summer. In fact, in early 1647, St. John's actions are astonishingly passive—those of a man who understood that he was no longer a principal player in the unfolding of events.

There is little evidence that St. John tried to prevent Holles from disbanding the Army. Bellievre, the French envoy in London, reported that, during the debates over the army, "the Independents who command it, did what they could to prevent it, but in vain; the Presbyterians carried it with a large majority."[15] Bellievre, however, did not name St. John, so there is no direct evidence to demonstrate St. John's opposition. In fact, St. John's only recorded activities in January 1647, when the debates over the Army commenced, involved his effort to settle the estates of the marquis of Winchester.[16] In addition, leadership of the group formerly led by St. John and Vane seems to have passed at least temporarily to Haselrig and Evelyn, who provided the active opposition to Holles, while both St. John and Vane retired from the front lines of politics.[17]

It is quite possible that St. John's retirement from politics in the first half of 1647 occurred because he and perhaps Vane cut some sort of a deal with Holles to allow Holles to proceed with disbanding the Army. This possibility is certainly plausible.[18] With his views on law and the Constitution, St. John could not have been enthusiastic about military rule, and he had in the past absented himself from the House of Commons at particularly tense moments. There is, unfortunately, no direct evidence to indicate that St. John and Holles negotiated a deal by which St. John agreed not to oppose the disbanding of the Army. And one other troubling question remains. If St. John reneged on promises made to Holles, Holles certainly would have blasted St. John's duplicity even further on this issue in his *Memoirs.*

One man, however, in 1647 was certain that St. John, along with Vane and Cromwell, had betrayed the Army. In February 1647, John Lilburne accused St. John and Vane, "those worldly wise prudential men," of leading Cromwell—who had also stood by while Holles disbanded the Army—"around by the nose."[19]

Another pamphlet, *Westminster Projects,* written according to Lilburne, by John Wildman, charged that St. John, Vane, Cromwell, Say, Fiennes, Wharton, and the rest "now oppressed the people" and designed to take government into their own hands, "not for a year, but forever." Wildman further alleged that the Independents failed to remove Holles and the Presbyterians from Parliament in June as the Army had demanded and even favored the Presbyterians over the Levellers.[20] By September 1647, Lilburne identified St. John, Vane, Say, and Wharton as "those four sons of Machiavelli," who, he bitterly sneered, "never in their lives stood further from the just liberty of the Commons of England, than might help them to pull down those great men that stood in the way of their own preferment."[21] Elsewhere, St. John was described as a "corrupt lawyer" and a "pettifogger for Independency."[22] To earn the contempt of both Holles and Lilburne in 1647 was a prodigious feat.

Lilburne's charges, while clearly exaggerated, nevertheless had substance. On a personal level, St. John made no attempt to rescue Lilburne from the Tower, which Lilburne naturally resented. On a political level, St. John clearly absented himself from Parliament while the crucial debates were in progress. He may have concluded a deal with Holles, as some have suggested, but it is much more likely that St. John simply recognized that the winds of politics were blowing strongly in Holles's favor, and that the ideas Holles was promoting were close to his own.

With the same acuity that perceived the coming of Holles's dominance, St. John reentered politics in July 1647 and adroitly aligned himself with the Army. Although there is no indication that St. John wished to thwart Holles's attempt to recover power, Holles later claimed that St. John arranged for Independent MPs to take refuge with the Army in July. St. John may have helped persuade Speaker Lenthall to abandon the chair. Lenthall's recollection did not specifically name St. John, but the speaker did recall that "Cromwell and his agents deceived a wiser man than myself; that excellent king and then might deceive me also; and so they did. I knew the Presbyterians would never restore the King to his just rights; these men swore they would."[23]

On 4 August, St. John subscribed to the Engagement pledging him to live and die with the army. On 6 August, Vane, assisted by another officer, John Lambert, presented to the Commons the "Heads of the Proposals," which had been drafted by Henry Ireton. This document contained provisions for religious toleration and a powerful Council of State, but, overall, it conceded a great deal to the King. The "Heads of the Proposals" would have allowed Charles to retain legislative veto, deprived him of control of the militia for a mere ten years, and permitted the survival of a noncoercive episcopacy.[24] That St. John might have been involved in drafting a proposal more generous to the King than the "Newcastle Propositions" is suggested by a remark Sir Edward Ford made regarding Cromwell and Ireton. According to Ford, Cromwell and Ireton had recently "spoken much in the King's behalf, seconded by Young Harry Vane, Mr. Solicitor, and Mr. Fiennes."[25] By September, Lilburne and John Wildman claimed to have discerned a "Cabinet Council" of "Grandees," which included Cromwell, Ireton, Vane, St. John, Say, Nathaniel Fiennes, Evelyn, and Pierrepoint. These men, Lilburne claimed, "now steer the affairs of the whole kingdom." Even if they did not "steer" the affairs of the kingdom, they did successfully oppose Martin's Vote of No Addresses to the King in late September.[26]

In one sense the Army's entry into politics recreated the middle group and greatly complicated the chances for settlement. In 1646 and for most of 1647 politics was dominated by the interplay between the parties led by St. John and Holles. But by September 1647 the number of interest groups had increased, as St. John found himself wedged between the king and Holles on one side and the Army, the Levellers, and parliamentary radicals on the other. Like Pym in 1642–43, St. John desired a settlement that would include Charles as a limited, but fairly strong monarch. But, unlike Pym, St. John could no longer command a wide range of support. Contemporaries, both English and Scottish, had long seen through the elaborate smoke screen behind the policies leading to the creation of the New Model Army and the eventual abandonment of the Scots. In the fall of 1647, St. John retained some influence among the "Grandees" and some peripheral power through his friendship with Cromwell, but not much else. Holles, the Scots, and Lilburne despised and mistrusted him, and the entry of the Army into politics reduced St. John from a man who created events to one who was forced to react to them.

Nevertheless, between June and September 1647, St. John pulled off a remarkable coup. During the first half of 1647, St. John had been swept away by the Holles onslaught, standing aside while Holles challenged the Army. In July 1647 he correctly recognized that if he wished to remain in politics he must choose between Holles and the Army. Although Holles's policies were by no means completely abhorrent to him, St. John chose the Army. By September he had regained enough influence so that he was contributing to the formulation of solutions intended to restore the monarchy.

But St. John was now merely a survivor. The period of his own ascendancy was over, and he had been superseded, first by Holles and now by the Army. His survival or success now emanated less from his political skills than from a barrel of a gun. To a degree the Revolution had left St. John behind. A major reason for St. John's ability to stand in the mainstream of political activity from 1637 to 1646 was that he was a forceful and erudite advocate of the most widely embraced constitutional ideas of the day. Beginning with Ship Money, St. John stood, with occasional deviations, for the rights of English citizens, the authority of Parliament, and the supremacy of the law and Constitution, as he conceived them. In 1647 the Levellers posed a formidable challenge to St. John's beliefs. Lilburne had already charged Parliament with tyranny, and in *The Just Man's Justification* he denounced the Magna Carta as a Norman innovation imposed by the tyrannical successors of William the Conqueror.[27] Richard Overton derided the Magna Carta as a "beggarly thing," and William Walwyn dismissed it as an inadequate statement of English rights because it was the work of a Norman. Demanding liberty of conscience and the equality of all before the law, the Levellers represented those who believed that the civil war had been fought to create a new order embodying these ideas, but discovered that it had brought only higher taxes, fresh abuses of power, and economic depression. Lilburne, Overton, and Walwyn had thus recognized that continued adherence to an Ancient Constitution protected Parliament, monarchy, and aristocratic dominance, at the same time precluding the kinds of changes they desired.

Believing that the Grandees had gained control, the Levellers mounted a campaign for the Army's soul. The centerpiece of this campaign was the famous *The Case of the Army Truly Stated,* published in October 1647. *The Case* reiterated most of the Army's previous grievances and endeavored to situate those grievances in a broader context of discontent, suggesting that the Army was the last line of defense against the tyranny of either the King or the Grandees. After the Army's actions in the summer of 1647, its commanders felt compelled to address the issues raised in *The Case,* and they moved swiftly to summon a general council, which began deliberations at Putney on 28 October.

In the fall of 1647, St. John and Cromwell were seemingly proceeding toward settlement along parallel lines. While St. John and the Grandees tried to hammer out a permanent settlement that would include the King, Cromwell made a three-hour speech defending the monarchy at Putney on 28 October. In addition to discussing *The Case of the Army Truly Stated,* the Army Council had also taken up discussion of the *Agreement of the People,* the most precise statement yet of Leveller principles.[28] The *Agreement* argued that, since the people possessed supreme power, Parliament ought to be made representative of them and prevented from acting in certain areas. Contending for a wide franchise, the *Agreement* further argued that even the poorest were only bound by their own consent.[29] In reply Henry Ireton insisted that the franchise must remain vested in property ownership to preserve order, and he concluded that Leveller principles could end only in "anarchy."[30]

Fear of radical ideas continued to mount during the fall of 1647. When the Army Council rejected the *Agreement,* angry soldiers paraded at Corkbush Field with copies of the *Agreement* pinned to their hats. Cromwell quickly quashed this display of insubordination and had one of the ringleaders shot. The Corkbush Field mutiny and its aftermath could only have enhanced the King's bargaining power. Yet, Charles continued to display his facility for the timely blunder. After some discussion with Ireton and the Army council of officers, Charles had seemingly agreed to a new settlement, the *Heads of the Proposals*. Three days after the Corkbush Field mutiny, however, Charles escaped parliamentary custody and fled to the Isle of Wight.

Undaunted, the middle group undertook an attempt to rescue the monarchy. On 27 October 1647 the Lords and the Commons voted to present Charles with a measure entitled the *Four Bills* as a precondition to settlement. St. John was on the final drafting committee and was a strong advocate of the course it proposed.[31] In return for his restoration, Charles was to grant Parliament control of the militia for twenty years, annul all past claims against Parliament, revoke all royal grants, and accept Parliament's right to adjourn itself. St. John's support for the *Four Bills* most likely reflects his belief that, as of 1647, the monarchy had to be preserved, even if the monarch could not be trusted.

Charles, however, rejected the *Four Bills,* and, on 27 December 1647, he signed an engagement with the Scots, agreeing to give Presbyterian Church government a three-year trial in return for Scottish military assistance. The Commons erupted in anger at Charles's actions. In early January 1648 the chambers rang with angry speeches denouncing both Charles and the monarchy.[32]

No longer able to manage Parliament, the moderates resorted to negotiating with the Scots in an attempt to undermine their alliance with the King. In all probability a new war would destroy any chance of a moderate settlement. Evelyn and Say were added to the Committee of Both Kingdoms, which, with the retirement of the Scots, was now called the Derby House Committee. The Committee dispatched four commissioners to Edinburgh to treat with the Scots. Two of them, William Ashhurst and Robert Goodwin, were middle-group

Presbyterians. A third, John Birch, was a Presbyterian in both religion and politics. Only the last, Brian Stapleton, was a radical. The commissioners, however, were only figureheads. Say, St. John, and Pierrepoint guided the course of action taken by the negotiators. Once in Scotland, the negotiators tried to stall the Scots by the "direction of Lord Say, Mr. Pierrepoint, and Sir [sic] Oliver St. John, and others, with whom they held joint correspondence and from them received continual instructions."[33]

The moderates also deployed new strategies to come to terms with Charles. Say, perhaps the most dedicated pursuer of the King, vanished from the political scene in March 1648, intending, it was rumored, to go to the Isle of Wight and bargain with Charles.[34] At the end of March, Say met with the other middle-group leaders, St. John, Pierrepoint, and Evelyn, at Wallingford. On the 31st, Evelyn, Pierrepoint, and St. John dined with Bulstrode Whitelocke. A correspondent of the earl of Lanark reported that the group decided that their interests were best served by concluding a treaty with the King, in an effort to "disengage" him from the Scots. On his return to London, Say buttonholed members of several factions trying to generate support for such a treaty.[35]

The dreams of settlement entertained by St. John and Say, however, collapsed quickly. In April 1648 news that the Scots were raising an army reached Westminster. Parliament reacted with war hysteria. Weeping members confessed that they had sinned by believing that the King was a man they could reason with, and they now resolved to bring him to his knees.[36] The threat of war had once again ruined the designs of St. John and Say. The coming of the second civil war further polarized the Commons, and St. John and Say found it impossible to maintain any coalition of moderates, radicals, and the Army. The atmosphere in the Commons was ominous. After a heated debate on 28 April the Commons resolved, 165–99, that it would not alter the fundamental government of the kingdom: the King, the Lords, and the Commons.[37] The passage of this proposal is not surprising. What is astonishing, however, is the size of the minority. Ninety-nine members were willing to reject the Ancient Constitution, perhaps yet another signal to St. John that his time had passed.

By casting his fortunes with the Scots, Charles made yet another tactical blunder. Plagued by recruiting woes and internal bickering, the Scottish Army did not cross the border into England until July 1648. Indecisive command allowed Cromwell first to subdue the rebellion in South Wales and then to rout the numerically superior Scots at Preston in August.

The period after Cromwell's victory at Preston was dominated by the abortive negotiations between the King and Parliament begun at Newport on 15 September. Once again, military intervention and civil war had a divisive effect on members. On the one hand, Cromwell regarded the second civil war as further evidence of Charles's boundless duplicity, and he further considered his victory at Preston as an additional sign of divine favor. On the other hand, many members, particularly Say, were led once again to sober reflection on their reliance on military power, and, consequently, they began advocating immediate settlement with the king. Taking a role assumed by Holles in 1646–47, Say spoke for those who were dismayed by increasing popular resentment of high taxes, the presence of dangerous radical groups threatening the social order, and the realization that Parliament was poised on the brink of having to decide between royal or military tyranny.

Say's positions were almost identical to those supported by St. John. Say advocated that Charles surrender militia power, subject his ministers to parliamentary approval with Royalists disqualified, and abolish episcopacy. But he also desired a return to monarchy, order, and legality. Although it is doubtful that Say and his supporters believed that Charles could be trusted, they clearly perceived a greater threat in their own allies than in the king.

Both Say and Cromwell sought St. John's support in the fall of 1648. On 1 September, Cromwell wrote affectionately to St. John, expressing hope that Vane would join them and concluding with greetings to Pierrepoint, Evelyn, and "the rest of our good friends."[38] A few weeks later, Say lobbied hard for St. John's support, assuring him at a "private junto" that if they did not now agree with his majesty . . . they were the bloodiest men alive, and for his part he would be for his majesty."[39]

Under pressure from both Cromwell and Say, St. John took an opportunity to retire from politics by accepting the position of Chief Justice of the Common Pleas Court. St. John was confirmed by the Commons on 12 October and sworn in on 22 November. Chief justices traditionally did not attend Parliament and remained aloof from politics, so St. John's acceptance of the appointment afforded him a graceful way of avoiding the difficult decisions on the near horizon. His role had been diminishing since early 1647, anyway, and two other examples further demonstrate his alienation from politics. He was still a member of the Committee of Safety, but he attended only 16 of the 319 meetings in the first year of its existence.[40] More significantly, he broke with Cromwell over Pride's Purge and refused to act as a judge at Charles's trial.[41] Given his labors for a settlement that would have included the king, and his reputation as a man of law, it is not hard to see why St. John refused to serve at the king's trial.

There is no direct evidence indicating the reasons for St. John's retirement from politics. Even contemporary news sheets, usually full of rumor and innuendo, are silent on this matter. We can, therefore, only speculate. By 1648 the Revolution had clearly reached a stage where St. John was unable to understand or master it. The English Civil War began as a dispute among the ruling classes regarding the extent to which parliamentary authority could be used to protect liberty and property from an obviously arbitrary monarch. After the outbreak of civil war, parliamentary leaders realized that defeating the King would require the participation of a broader base of people than many of them were willing to tolerate. As long as combating unrestrained monarchical authority was the preeminent issue, and traditional views of political sociability remained operative, St. John was able to maintain a firm grip on events. But with the end of the first civil war in 1646, the radical impulse emanating from the Army and the Levellers threatened the social order that St. John (as much as Holles) wished to preserve. In the face of radical ideas and military force, the constitutional solution once espoused by St. John was obsolete. In the end Cromwell forcibly stopped the radical drift of the Revolution, but only at the expense of implementing military rule.

Conclusion

The events leading up to Pride's Purge concluded St. John's effective participation in the Great Rebellion. Most historians believe that his role after 1649 was less consequential than it had been previously.[1] More problematic, however, St. John extended his highly refined talent for elusiveness and clandestine behavior. Studying his activities and discerning his motivations after 1649 becomes an exercise in intellectual masochism. Men who come to merit a nickname, as St. John did as the "dark lantern" of the Protectorate, acquire such titles because they are circumspect in their behavior and are unusually careful not to leave evidence of their activities behind. This study, tracing his career up to 1649, has bordered on becoming a "life and times." A study of St. John's career after 1649 becomes almost exclusively a life and times (and often more times than life), adding little to existing knowledge.

The outline, if not the details and shadings of St. John's post-1649 career, however, is fairly clear. It is evident that he wished to play only a minor role in politics immediately after 1649. His next major initiative concerned his negotiations, conducted with Walter Strickland in February 1651, with the Dutch regarding a possible economic and political union between England and the United Provinces. The Dutch were uninterested in the political aspects of the scheme, and, when negotiations broke down, Whitelocke recorded that St. John, humiliated by the Dutch, arranged for his friends in the Rump Parliament to obtain his recall to England.[2] On 27 June 1651, Parliament rescinded its vote of October 1649, prohibiting judges from holding seats in Parliament while they were still in office. This action allowed St. John to return to his seat in Parliament. Two months later the Committee for the Reformation of the Universities appointed him chancellor of Cambridge University, and he was one of eight commissioners sent to Scotland to discuss a union between the two countries.[3]

In his few political statements he stressed the need for "something of monarchical power" to maintain land and liberty.[4] But he also expressed a distaste for "Cromwell and the Army." St. John also did not appear to have been pleased by the formation of the Protectorate.

He rejected Cromwell's offer of a place on the Council of State and, according to Thurloe, performed only his judicial duties, fleeing to his country house at the end of each term. To a degree his lethargy may be explained by his later assertion that he was seriously ill from October 1653 until May 1654, hovering, as he claimed later, near death.[5] But even after his recovery, he refused to participate in the Protectorate. Defending his behavior in 1660, he declared that "I never would come to his [Cromwell's] council or sit in the other house. He made me one of the commissioners of the treasury. I never intermeddled or received salary either as a councillor or commissioner; I, nor any of my relations, never had one penny advantage by them, or by his means, directly or indirectly, save the continuance of my place as a judge."[6]

St. John also was indifferent to Richard Cromwell's assumption of power. He resumed his seat in Parliament when the Rump was restored in 1659, an action that squares with his post-Restoration claim that he recognized only the Parliament summoned by Charles I in 1640. On 7 February 1660, Samuel Pepys reported that "my Lord St. John is for a free Parliament and that he is very great with Monck."[7] At the Restoration, he fled, doubtless at Monck's contrivance, to his estate in Northamptonshire, suffering only the penalty of perpetual disbarment from office. Edmund Ludlow reported that St. John's escape aroused the great disappointment of Charles II.[8] In 1662, St. John fled to Basle and later to Augsburg, and he died in exile on 31 December 1673.

In 1660, St. John composed a brief apologia, *The Case of Oliver St. John.* It is a much different document from Holles's memoir. Whereas Holles was determined to blacken the character of his opponents, St. John devoted himself primarily to justifying his own behavior, dissociating himself from Cromwell, and contending that he had nothing to do with Charles I's execution nor had he served in any Parliament not summoned by Charles I.[9] Such arguments, of course, depended on pure sophistry. It was true that St. John had not participated in Charles's execution, but he certainly was one of the men most responsible for placing Charles in a position where he could be brought to trial. St. John's protests about not serving Cromwell would have carried more conviction if he had also resigned his position as chief justice. But constructing his defense in this manner did enable St. John to focus on the strongest part of his case: his behavior in the year before Pride's Purge, during which time he could portray himself with some justice as a defender of the monarchy.

The career of Oliver St. John represents the dilemma of the constitutional opponent of Charles I's policies and ministers. Like many Americans in the 1980s, St. John was often ideologically conservative but operationally liberal, and he sought a political system that could restrain the policies of Charles I without threatening the social fabric of society. The Ship Money case provided St. John with a cause he would plead many times in the next few years. One suspects that, to a degree, his personal bitterness over losing a case that he believed he deserved to win accounts for some of the urgency with which he pursued Ship Money in the Short and Long Parliaments. But there can also be little doubt that St. John considered Charles's attempt to intimidate the judiciary and impose new taxation without parliamentary consent to be the most serious problem facing the nation in 1640. His attacks on Ship Money and Finch place him firmly in what John Morrill has called the "constitutionalist-legalist perception of misgovernment."[10] Although St. John disliked the bishops, there is little indication that he subscribed to the idea that England's problems were caused by a Catholic conspiracy created either by the bishops or by Charles. On this score and several others as well, St. John departed from his colleague Pym.

St. John also departed from his constitutional principles when he became involved in the Strafford case. He took little part in the early stages of the trial, but when the Commons reverted to attainder in April 1641, St. John took up the fight with a vengeance. His speech to the Lords on 29 April 1641, however, sought to justify the attainder on the shakiest legal grounds. St. John faced a dilemma common to many revolutionaries: sometimes it is necessary to break the law in order to bring justice to those who have broken the law. Unlike several others who subscribed to the "constitutionalist-legalist" perception of misgovernment, St. John was seldom troubled by contradictions that accompanied this point of view.

In *The Case of Oliver St. John,* St. John, addressing himself only to his post-1648 activities, grounded his defense on the idea that he had nothing to do with Charles I's death and that he had supported only parliaments summoned by Charles I. This proposition is debatable, as we have just seen, but St. John could have made a similar case for his actions before 1648. Consistently in the months before the civil war, St. John sought ways to render to Charles a compromise Root and Branch Bill, a compromise Militia Bill, and extended grants of tonnage and poundage. Clarendon bitterly inveighed against St. John for abusing the office of solicitor. Although St. John was certainly not Charles's most loyal servant, he did work harder in the king's behalf than he has been given credit for. It is astonishing, but probably not as astonishing as some have suggested, that Charles did not replace him as solicitor until 1643.

St. John was clearly distressed by the choice being forced on him in

1642. He contributed little to the debates in the spring of 1642 and agonized over joining Charles in York, but in the end he remained with Parliament. We have few windows into St. John's mind at any time, but our information is particularly scanty as the outbreak of the civil war approached. What factors weighed in St. John's decision? We can only speculate, but it is hard to imagine the committed defender of the Constitution and judiciary throwing his lot with a king he regarded as a menace to the legal foundation of England.

Once St. John cast his lot with Parliament, he recognized the truth of the earl of Manchester's aphorism: "If we fight the king a hundred times and beat him ninety nine times, yet he is King still. But if he beat us once, or the last time we shall all be hanged, we shall lose our estates, and our posterities shall be undone."[11] St. John did not accept Manchester's conclusion, but he did believe defeat had to be avoided at all costs. In conjunction with Pym, he campaigned for an alliance with the Scots that would tip the military balance in Parliament's favor. St. John was determined that Charles not be allowed to win a decisive military victory and that any settlement protect men like himself, who had taken the parliamentary side and feared reprisals in the event of a Royalist victory.

St. John's most visible contributions to the war effort occurred after Pym's death in 1643. First, he succeeded Pym as parliamentary leader, transforming himself from an occasional ideologue into a practical man of politics. He concluded an alliance with the Scots and took the lead in persuading the Commons to pass the Solemn League and Covenant. Second, whereas Pym had been a master of compromise, St. John contributed mightily to the first real divisive change in the nature of parliamentary politics. During the time Pym dominated the House of Commons, few religious divisions of any consequence emerged in Parliament. Puritans of varying shades of commitment and conviction, such as Pym and St. John, were united under the appellation of the "Godly Party." Hostility toward the Scots and Presbyterians as well as the acceptance of the earl of Essex as a commander were widely accepted. The fortunes of war, however, slowly eroded the unity of the "Godly Party." Essex's failure to conduct the war in an aggressive and competent manner combined with the passage of the Solemn League and Covenant to introduce new and divisive elements into the Commons. When Essex surrendered his army at Lostwithiel, one of the liberal opportunities for a Puritan consensus in the House of Commons vanished.

To break the grim deadlock, St. John undertook measure after measure to purge the New Model Army of aristocratic commanders, to retain Scottish support without making concessions to State Presbyterians, and to install a more active fighting force. When the Army at last won a decisive victory to ensure the protection of the parliamentary cause, St. John dumped the Scots as ignominiously as he had dumped Essex.

The Army's great victories came at a still-higher cost. In the course of fulfilling its national mission of defeating the King, the Army developed a distinct political consciousness, and many members decided that the Army posed a threat potentially as dangerous as the King. In early 1647, Denzil Holles seized on the opportunity provided by the scattered threads of distrust and trepidation surrounding the Army's emergence. Forging an unholy and short-lived alliance between parliamentary moderates, the Scots, and the City of London, Holles tried to disband the Army. Ironically, Holles was as Erastian as St. John and was as insincere toward the Scots as St. John had been in 1643, and yet, in his *Memoirs,* Holles castigated St. John for his treachery against the Scots. But equally ironic, St. John, who did nothing to prevent Holles from trying to destroy the Army, fled to the Army in August 1647 and became allied with its leadership. St. John had probably been as interested in Holles in reducing the Army's power. Like Frankenstein, he had seen his creation grow into a many-headed monster.

Finally, the introduction of radical ideas, sometimes more hostile to the Parliament than the King, sealed the end of St. John's effective participation as a political operative. Despite his occasional departures from legality and due process, St. John remained a Parliament man and a defender of the traditional order of government. By 1648, to men like Lilburne, adherence to such principles meant continued parliamentary tyranny. Like Holles, St. John was never able to adjust to changing times, remaining tied to ideas about the Constitution that were operative in 1640–42 but that were obsolete in 1648.

In one respect the history of the English Civil War can be traced by locating the points at which the conflict became too radical for some of the original parliamentary figures. For Digby the point of no return came with the trial of Strafford. For Clarendon and Culpepper it was the Grand Remonstrance. For Holles it was the first engagement of the civil war. For St. John the moment of truth came much later, when he came to fear the power of the Army and the radicalism of the Levellers as much as he feared a royal tyranny. As participants in the civil war, such as Clarendon and Holles, began to reflect on the events of the 1640s, St. John was perhaps unfairly villified in their accounts. He was the only one of the original core leaders who survived the 1640s and who also could be blamed for the course the war had taken. Hampden's death at Chalgrove field, Pym's illness, and Holles's conservatism spared them the full fury of retrospective judgment. Even though he was judged very harshly by his contemporaries, St. John was at heart a moderate conservative, committed to traditional forms of political sociability, to Parliament, and to the monarchy. But moderates—Crane Brinton instructed us long ago—lose to radicals during the course of a rebellion. St. John was no exception.[12]

Notes

Abbreviations

B.L.   British Library
B.I.H.R.   *Bulletin of the Institute of Historical Research*
C.S.P.   *Calendar of State Papers*
E.H.R.   *English Historical Review*
H.J.   *Historical Journal*
J.B.S.   *Journal of British Studies*
J.M.H.   *Journal of Modern History*

Introduction

1. Mary Frear Keller lists fifteen biographies of Cromwell in her *Bibliography of British History, Stuart Period* (Oxford, 1970). In the 1990s, new studies, written by Barry Coward and edited by John Morrill have appeared. There are three major studies of Pym, including those by C. E. Wade, S. Read Brett, and J. H. Hexter.

2. See H. F. Adams and J. F. Folland, *Sir Henry Vane the Younger* (Boston, 1973); and Violet Rowe, *Sir Henry Vane the Younger* (London, 1970); John Adair, *A Life of John Hampden: The Patriot* (London, 1976).

3. Patricia Crawford, *Denzil Holles, 1598–1689: A Study of His Political Career* (London, 1979).

4. See the unpublished doctoral dissertation by C. M. Williams, "The Political Career of Henry Marten" (Oxford University, D. Phil. thesis, 1954), and Raymond Stearns, *The Strenuous Puritan* (Urbana, 1954).

5. Ruth Spalding, *The Improbable Puritan* (London, 1975).

6. Valerie Pearl, "Oliver St. John and the Middle Group in the Long Parliament, August 1643–May 1644," *English Historical Review* 81 (1966): 490–519.

7. Oliver St. John, "Mr. St. John's Speech on the Attainder of the Earl of Strafford," B. L. Thomason, E 708 (7), p. 72.

8. Alan Everitt, *The Community of Kent and the Great Rebellion 1640–1660* (Leicester, 1966); John Morrill, *The Revolt of the Provinces: Conservatives and Radicals in the English Civil War 1630–1650*, 2d ed. (London, 1980). For a different view, see Clive Holmes, "The County Community in Early Stuart Historiography," *Journal of British Studies* 19 (1980): 54–73.

9. Patrick Collinson, *The Religion of Protestants* (Oxford, 1982); Nicholas Tyacke, *Anti-Calvinists: The Rise of English Arminianism, c. 1590–1640* (Oxford, 1987); John Morrill, "The Religious Context of the English Civil War," *Transactions of the Royal Historical Society*, 5th ser., vol. 34 (1984): 155–78.

10. Conrad Russell, "Parliamentary History in Perspective, 1603–29," *History* 61 (1976): 1–27; Kevin Sharpe, "Parliamentary History 1603–1629: In or Out of Perspective?" in Kevin Sharpe, ed., *Faction and Parliament: Essays on Early Stuart*

History, 2d ed. (London, 1985): 1–42. Russell's views on the 1640s are now appearing. See his *The Causes of the English Civil War* (Oxford, 1990).

11. Perez Zagorin, "Did Strafford Change Sides?" *English Historical Review* 101 (1986), p. 151, n. 1. Readers of this article will note my debt to Zagorin's fair and concise summary of the revisionist position in this entire paragraph.

12. Anthony Fletcher, *The Outbreak of the English Civil War* (New York, 1981); Caroline Hibbard, *Charles I and the Popish Plot* (Chapel Hill, N.C., 1983); and Morrill, "The Religious Context."

13. Mark Kishlansky, *The Rise of the New Model Army* (Cambridge, 1979); and idem., "The Emergence of Adversary Politics in the Long Parliament," *Journal of Modern History* 49 (1977): 617–40.

14. There are now many critiques of revisionist historiography. For several of the most incisive, see J. H. Hexter, "Power Struggle, Parliament and Liberty in Early Stuart England," *Journal of Modern History* 50 (1978): 1–50; idem., "The Early Stuarts and Parliament: Old Hat and the *Nouvelle Vague,*" *Parliamentary History* 1 (1982): 181–125; Derek Hirst, "Unanimity in the Commons, Aristocratic Intrigues, and the Origins of the English Civil War," *JMH* 50 (1978): 51–71; idem., "The Place of Principle," *Past and Present* 91 (1981): 79–99. For a recent critique, see Michael Finlayson, *Historians, Puritanism, and the English Revolution* (Toronto, 1983).

15. B.L. Add Mss. 14827, fol. 123.

16. Oliver St. John, *The Case of Oliver St. John Concerning His Actions during the Late Troubles,* B.L. E 1035 (5), pp. 6–7.

17. St. John did compose a brief apologia (cited in n. 16), but it lacks the passion and acerbity of Holles's memoirs, and it deals almost entirely with events after 1649 in which St. John was not as important as he had been before 1649.

18. Judith Maltby, ed., *The Short Parliament Diary of Sir Thomas Aston* (London, 1988); Willson H. Coates, Anne Steele Young, and Vernon F. Snow, *The Private Journals of the Long Parliament* (New Haven, 1982); Vernon F. Snow and Anne Young, *The Private Journals of the Long Parliament: 7 March to 1 June 1642* (New Haven, 1987); and Margaret F. Stieg, ed., *The Diary of John Harington, M.P., 1646–53* (Old Woking, Surrey, 1977).

19. Clarendon, *History* 1: 246–7.

20. Ibid., 3: 470.

21. Robert Baillie, *The Letters and Journals of Robert Baillie,* 3 vols. (Edinburgh, 1841–42), 2: 133.

22. Bulstrode Whitelocke, *Memorials of the English Affairs,* 4 vols. (Oxford, 1853), 2: 453.

23. *Mercurius Britannicus,* 4 January 1644–11 January 1644; B. L. Thomason, E. 81 (20), p. 154.

24. John Lilburne, "Jonah's Cry Out of the Whale's Belly," B.L. Thomason, E 400 (30), p. 3.

25. *Mercurius Elenticus,* 1 March 1647–8 March 1647.

26. *Mercurius Pragmaticus* 13 June 1648–20 June 1648, B. L. Thomason, E. 448 (7), p. 6.

27. Denzil Holles, *Memoirs of Denzil, Lord Holles,* in Frances Maseres, ed., *Select Tracts Relating to the Civil Wars in England* (London, 1815), p. 189.

28. Two particularly good descriptions of source problems may be found in Hexter, *Reign of King Pym,* pp. 51–54, and Kishlansky, *The New Model,* pp. ix–x.

29. J. P. Kenyon, *Stuart England* (London, 1978), p. 126; Hexter, *Reign of King Pym,* p. 163; S. R. Gardiner, *History of the Great Civil Wars* 4 vols. (London, 1893), 1: 304; and Robert Ashton, *The English Civil War: Conservatism and Revolution, 1603–1649* (London, 1979), p. 237.

30. Thomas Mason, *Serving God and Mammon: William Juxon, 1582–1663, Bishop of London, Lord High Treasurer of England, and Archbishop of Canterbury* (Newark, Del., 1985), p. 135–36. I am grateful to Martin Havran for his reference.

31. John Lilburne, "Letter to John Goodwin," B.L. Thomason, E 400 (5), p. 6.

32. See the discussion of Sieyes in J. M. Thompson, *Leaders of the French Revolution* (Oxford, 1929), pp. 3–16. I do not suggest that the two men were exactly alike. Sieyes, of course, was a Catholic priest.

33. A. J. P. Taylor, "Accident Prone, or What Happened Next?" *JMH* 49 (1977): 11.

34. In addition to Pearl's *EHR* article, cited in note 6, see Valerie Pearl, "The 'Royal Independents' in the English Civil War," *Transactions of the Royal Historical Society*, 5th ser. vol. 18 (1968): 69–96.

Chapter 1. Theme and Variations

1. *D.N.B*, 17: 640–1. A recent brief sketch of St. John's early life may be found in J. R. MacCormack, *Revolutionary Politics in the Long Parliament* (Cambridge, Mass., 1973), p. 2.

2. S. R. Gardiner (ed.), *Documents Relating to the Proceedings Against William Prynne in 1634 and 1637* (London, 1876), p. xxv. See also Irvonwy Morgan, *Prince Charles' Puritan Chaplain* (London, 1957).

3. Ibid. For a closer look at the inns, see Wilfred R. Prest, *The Inns of Court under Elizabeth I and the Early Stuarts, 1590–1640* (London, 1972).

4. A. P. Newton, *The Colonizing Activities of the English Puritans* (New Haven, 1914), p. 65.

5. Clarendon, *History*, 1: 246. Actually, the "design" was a copy of Sir Robert Dudley's tract, *Proposition for His Majesty's Service to Bridle the Impertinence of Parliaments*. For a general discussion of its contents, see Rushworth, *Historical Collections*, 2: 51–53.

6. Clarendon, *History*, 1: 246.

7. Ibid. Much has been made of the complicated connections between participants in the Revolution. Bedford and the republican Haselrig were related by marriage. Of Lord Saye's children, one married the oppositionist earl of Lincoln; the other married the son of the Dorset oppositionist Walter Earle. Saye's younger son, Nathaniel Fiennes, was Sir John Eliot's son-in-law. Connected by marriage to the Barringtons were Hampden, St. John, Gilbert Gerrard, Oliver Warwick and Denzil Holles, and he addressed Pym as "brother." See B. L. Egerton Mss. 2645, fols. 120, 126, 154, 170, and 186. Still, too much must not be made of these relationships. After all, many of the men ended up on opposite sides during the Revolution. Years ago, J. H. Hexter warned of the mistakes that can occur from trying to construct arguments from connections. See his *Reign of King Pym* (Cambridge, Mass., 1941), pp. 73–75.

8. Clarendon, *History*, 1: 246.

9. Newton, *Colonizing Activities*, p. 57.

10. Ibid. p. 56.

11. Ibid., p. 3. Oliver Cromwell took no part in the company's activities, but he most likely was acquainted with them. His aunt, Joan Barrington, was the mother of Thomas Barrington, and he was a friend of the earl of Warwick.

12. P.R.O., C.O. 124, fol. 2.

13. Ibid. See also Newton, *Colonizing Activities*, p. 60.

14. St. John is called the company lawyer in several places in the surviving

documents of the company. However, neither the two folio volumes preserved in the Public Record Office or in the *Calendar of State Papers, Colonial, 1574–1660* records specific cases that St. John handled in behalf of the company. His one recorded litigation for the company, the case of Capt. Philip Bell in 1638, will be discussed later.

15. B. L. Egerton Mss., fols. 120, 126, 154, 170, and 186.

16. Huntingdonshire Record Office, Manchester Mss., 19/3/2. Cited in Conrad Russell, "Land Sales, 1540–1640: A Comment on the Evidence," in the *Economic History Review,* 2d Ser. vol. 25, no. 1 (February 1972), pp. 117–21.

17. Abbott, *Cromwell,* 1: 102. For more on the background and opposition to the fen drainage schemes, see H. C. Darby, *The Draining of the Fens,* 2d ed. (Cambridge, 1956); Margaret Albright, "The Entrepreneurs of Fen Drainage in England under James I and Charles I: An Illustration of the Uses of Influence," *Explorations in Entrepreneurial History* 8 (1955–56): 51–65; *The Agrarian History of England and Wales,* vol. 4, ed. Joan Thirsk (Cambridge, 1967); and Keith Lindley, *Fenland Riots and the English Revolution* (London, 1982).

18. Ibid.

19. Nor is anything known about St. John's role in the dispute that arose among the investors over the distribution of the lands.

20. His investments were not large, and few profits were made on the fens because of the ensuring legal battles. See W. G. Dugdale, *The History of the Imbanking and Draining of Divers Fens and Marshes* 2d ed., ed. Charles Nason Cole (London, 1772). Moreover, the land market itself was an uncertain road to wealth in the 1630s. See also Mark E. Kennedy, "Charles I and Local Government: The Draining of the East and West Fens," *Albion* 15, 1 (Spring, 1983): 19–31.

21. W. J. Jones, *Politics and the Bench: Judges and the Origins of the English Civil War* (London, 1971), p. 2.

22. Ibid., p. 124.

23. John Morrill, *The Revolt of the Provinces* (London, 1976), p. 22.

24. Ibid.

25. This period is now being reexamined extensively. See Esther S. Cope, *Politics without Parliaments, 1629–1640* (London, 1987); and L. J. Reeve, *Charles I and the Road to the Personal Rule* (Cambridge, 1989).

26. Kevin Sharpe, "The Personal Rule of Charles I," in Howard Tomlinson, ed., *Before the English Civil War* (London, 1983). For a different point of view, see Hugh F. Kearney, *The Eleven Years' Tyranny of Charles I* (London, 1962).

27. D. L. Keir, "The Case of Ship Money," *Law Quarterly Review* 52 (1936): 546–74; Adair, *Life of Hampden,* p. 109.

28. Ibid.

29. Rushworth, *Historical Collections,* 2: 257.

30. V. A. Rowe, "Robert, Earl of Warwick and the Payment of Ship Money," *Transactions of the Essex Archaeological Society,* 3d ser., 1 (1964–65): 160–63. See also M. D. Gordon, "The Collection of Ship Money in the Reign of Charles I," *Transactions of the Royal Historical Society,* 3d ser., 4 (1910): 141–62.

31. Jones, *Politics and the Bench.* See Document 24. Chief Justice Finch also was suspected of coercing several of the other judges.

32. Rushworth, *Historical Collections,* 2: 355.

33. For details on Hampden, see Adair, *Life of Hampden.* See also D. H. Pennington, "The Rebels of 1642," in R. H. Parry, ed., *The English Civil War and After, 1642–1658* (London, 1970), pp. 23–29.

34. Perez Zagorin, *The Court and the Country* (New York, 1971), p. 93.

35. Gardiner, *Documents Relating to Prynne,* pp. 77–78.

36. Ibid. Burton, Bastwick, and Prynne all were convinced opponents of divine right episcopacy. See William Lamont, *Marginal Prynne, 1600–1669* (London, 1963). There is no evidence of St. John's views on episcopacy at this time. By 1641, of course, he was an opponent of it.

37. Gardiner, *Documents Relating to Prynne*, pp. 82–83.

38. Ibid.

39. S. R. Gardiner, *History of England from the Accession of James I to the Outbreak of Civil War, 1603–1642* (New York, 1965), 8: 272.

40. Rushworth, *Historical Collections*, 2: 484.

41. Ibid., p. 508. See also Margaret Judson, *The Crisis of the Constitution* (New Brunswick, N.J., 1949), pp. 270–71.

42. J. G. A. Pocock, *The Ancient Constitution and the Feudal Law* (New York, 1967), pp. 50–56.

43. Rushworth, *Historical Collections*, 2: 525.

44. Rushworth, *Historical Collections*, 2: 527.

45. The crown was hesitant, of course, also because it was in the midst of dealing with Prynne, Burton, Bastwick, and John Lilburne. The religious fervor connected with these men may have convinced Charles that calling Parliament would have been a disaster. And he may have been right. For details on the Church and the problems posed by these men, see H. R. Trevor-Roper, *Archbishop Laud* (Cambridge, 1943).

46. St. John's most convincing precedents concerned the reign of Edward III. During the Hundred Years' War, Edward used Parliament to raise the money he needed to continue fighting. No previous king had cultivated Parliament so courteously. As a result St. John was able to cite numerous examples of Edward's going to Parliament in order to raise money for national defense. Edward's tactic of cultivating Parliament worked well for him as it did for most successful warrior kings in the Middle Ages, but it established precedents that were difficult for his successors to follow. Neither Richard II (1377–99) nor Henry IV (1399–1413) was successful at war, and both encountered difficulties managing a Parliament not used to high-handed methods. On another level St. John made little reference to the reigns of kings overthrown while in office. This situation would change in 1640 when St. John would devote considerable time to the reign of Richard II.

47. Rushworth, *Historical Collections* 2: 496.

48. This point is discussed in Judson, *Crisis of the Constitution*, p. 271.

49. C. V. Wedgwood, *The King's Peace, 1637–1641* (New York, 1955), p. 192.

50. For Coke and the Ancient Constitution, see Pocock, *The Ancient Constitution*, pp. 30–56.

51. Pocock, *The Ancient Constitution*. See also D. R. Kelley, *Foundations of Modern Historical Scholarship* (New York, 1970), for another view of the insularity of English lawyers. St. John was perhaps not as insular as Coke. He did cite Livy on one occasion, but Livy is not central to any part of his argument. It should be noted that not all English lawyers during this period were insular in outlook. See Hans S. Pawlisch, *Sir John Davies and the Conquest of Ireland: A Study in Legal Imperialism* (Cambridge, 1985).

52. Pocock, *The Ancient Constitution*, pp. 35, 50–56.

53. Gardiner, *History of England*, 8: 273–74.

54. St. John, despite talking for two days, actually was the most concise of the four men. Littleton talked for four days and Holborne for six. Attorney General Bankes concluded the trial with a three-day summation.

55. Gardiner, *History of England*, 8: 274.

56. Ibid.

57. Holborne also ably picked apart Littleton's arguments that Parliament could

not be called because there was not enough time. Holborne observed that Littleton's position had no relation to actual fact. The arguments of too little time made no sense because this was the fourth exaction of Ship Money and no attempt had yet been made to secure Parliament's consent.

58. Gardiner, *History of England,* 8: 275.

59. Twentieth-century researchers have, of course, reduced the amount of triumph associated with these events. See Sidney Painter, *The Reign of King John* (Baltimore, 1949); and F. M. Powicke, *The Thirteenth Century* (Oxford, 1959). Nevertheless, seventeenth-century observers regarded them as victories of right and justice. See Faith Thompson, *The Magna Carta and the English Constitution* (Minneapolis, 1961), and Maurice Ashley, *Magna Carta in Seventeenth Century England* (Charlottesville, 1965).

60. Wedgwood, *The King's Peace,* pp. 192–98.

61. Ibid., pp. 193–94.

62. Ibid., p. 194.

63. Gardiner, *Constitutional Documents,* pp. 121, 123.

64. Wedgwood, *The King's Peace,* pp. 205–6. See also the argument in Conrad Russell, "The Ship Money Judgments of Bramston and Davenport," *EHR* 302 (April 1962): 312–18.

65. It should be recorded, however, that two of the judges upholding Hampden did so on technical grounds. If legality is the only measure, the King's victory was actually nine to three.

66. Gardiner, *History of England,* 8: 280. The differences between the judges here reenforce the arguments in J. P. Sommerville, *Politics and Ideology in England 1603–1640* (London, 1986).

67. Ibid., p. 281.

68. Judson, *Crisis of the Constitution,* pp. 9–10. See also M. J. Mendle, "Politics and Political Thought," in Conrad Russell, ed., *The Origins of the English Civil War* (London, 1973), pp. 219–20.

69. Morrill, *Revolt of the Provinces.*

70. Derek Hirst, *Authority and Conflict: England 1603–1658* (Cambridge, Mass., 1986), p. 179.

71. Clarendon, *History,* 1: 89–90. For evidence that opposition to Ship Money spread beyond a small group of malcontents and into the county communities, see K. Fincham, "The Judges' Decision on Ship Money in February 1637: the Reaction of Kent," *BIHR,* 57 (1984): 230–37; and N. Jackson, "The Collection of Ship Money in Northamptonshire, 1635–40" (University of Birmingham, M. Phil., 1987), chapter 3.

72. William Laud, *The Works of William Laud,* ed. W. Scott and J. Bliss, 7 vols. (Oxford, 1847–60), 6: 42.

73. Wedgwood, *The King's Peace,* p. 193.

74. Jones, *Politics and the Bench,* p. 123.

75. Bulstrode Whitelocke, *Memorials of the English Affairs* (London, 1853), 1: 350.

76. J. E. Halliwell, ed., *The Autobiography and Correspondence of Sir Symonds D'Ewes* (London, 1845), 2: 129–36.

Chapter 2. Coming of Age in the Short and Long Parliaments

1. For recent assessments of Laudian policies, see Nicholas Tyacke, *Anti-Calvinists: The Rise of English Arminianism, c. 1590–1640* (Oxford, 1987); and

Charles Carlton, *Archbishop William Laud* (New York, 1987).

2. Lawrence Stone, *The Causes of the English Revolution, 1529–1642* (New York, 1972), p. 128; John Morrill, "The Religious Context of the English Civil War," *Transactions of the Royal Historical Society,* 5th ser. 34 (1984): 157.

3. Historians have come recently to recognize the critical importance of Scottish affairs in the events leading up to the Civil Wars. On the matter of the prayer book and canons, see Gordon Donaldson, *The Making of the Scottish Prayer Book of 1637* (Edinburgh, 1954); Maurice Lee, *The Road to Revolution: Scotland under Charles I, 1625–1637* (Urbana and Chicago, 1985); Conrad Russell, "The British Problem and the English Civil War," *History* 72 (October 1987): 395–415; and, most recently, Peter Donald, *An Uncounseled King; Charles I and the Scottish Troubles, 1637–1641* (Cambridge, 1991).

4. For Strafford, see H. F. Kearney, *Strafford in Ireland* (Manchester, 1959); see also C. V. Wedgwood, *Thomas Wentworth, the First Earl of Strafford, 1593–1641: A Revaluation* (London, 1961).

5. See W. C. Abbott, *Writings and Speeches of Oliver Cromwell* (Cambridge, Mass., 1937), 1: 96.

6. Abbott, *Cromwell,* 1: 96–97.

7. Ibid.

8. Ibid.

9. Ibid.

10. A. P. Newton, *The Colonizing Activities of the English Puritans* (New Haven, 1914), pp. 216–17.

11. Ibid., p. 218.

12. Ibid.

13. The arbitrators in the case were Bell's brother Robert and John Hampden.

14. Newton, *Colonizing Activities,* p. 219.

15. Clarendon, *History,* 1: 183.

16. E. S. Cope, *Proceedings in the Short Parliament* (London, 1977), pp. 148–49.

17. Ibid., p. 163. St. John's speech also is described by Thomas Aston in Judith D. Maltby, ed., *The Short Parliament Diary of Sir Thomas Aston* (London, 1988), p. 17.

18. Ibid.

19. Ibid., p. 168. See also Maltby, *Diary of Aston,* p. 31.

20. Ibid., pp. 176–79.

21. Ibid., p. 196.

22. Ibid., p. 209. Aston has a less precise version of St. John's speech, but he does note St. John's suggestion, made twice later in the day, that if Ship Money were laid aside by the king subsidies could be granted. See Maltby, *Diary of Aston,* pp. 134–45, 140.

23. C. V. Wedgwood, *The King's Peace, 1637–1641* (New York, 1955), p. 326.

24. Ivan Roots, *The Great Rebellion* (London, 1966), p. 2.

25. Clarendon, *History,* 1: 183.

26. Ibid.

27. Bodleian Library, 88*, fol. 117r; see also B.L. Add. Mss. 11045, fol. 115r.

28. Perez Zagorin, *The Court and the Country* (New York, 1971), p. 116. Recently, several works have cast light on the opening of the Long Parliament. See Anthony Fletcher, *The Outbreak of the English Civil War* (New York, 1981); Conrad Russell, "Why Did Charles Call the Long Parliament?" *History* 69 (October 1984): 375–83.

29. The problem of leadership is considered in Sheila Lambert, "The Opening of the Long Parliament," *Historical Journal* 27 (1984): 265–87.

30. Fletcher, *Outbreak of the Civil War,* pp. xix–xx; Zagorin, *Court and Country,* p. 201.

31. Clarendon, *History,* 1: 245.

32. Ibid., 1: 241.

33. The character and role of Bedford is discussed in Clayton Roberts, "The Earl of Bedford and the Coming of the English Civil War," *Journal of Modern History* 49 (December 1977): 600–616.

34. Clarendon, *History,* 1: 246.

35. Ibid.

36. Ibid., p. 247.

37. Notestein, *D'Ewes,* p. 42.

38. Ibid., p. 74.

39. Ibid., p. 172–74.

40. Ibid., p. 123.

41. Ibid., p. 152.

42. Ibid., pp. 154–55.

43. Ibid., p. 166.

44. John Northcote, *The Diary of John Northcote* (London, 1877), pp. 83–84.

45. C. V. Wedgwood, *The King's Peace, 1637–1641* (New York, 1955), pp. 381–82.

46. Notestein, *D'Ewes,* p. 253.

47. Oliver St. John, "Speech to the Lords Concerning Ship Money," B. L. Thomason, E 196 (1), p. 2.

48. Ibid., p. 27.

49. Ibid.

50. Clarendon, *History,* p. 280. See also the excellent discussion in Clayton Roberts, *Schemes and Undertakings* (Columbus, Ohio, 1985), pp. 31–56; and Conrad Russell, "Parliament and the King's Finances," in *The Origins of the English Civil War,* ed. Conrad Russell (London, 1973), pp. 91–116, especially pp. 110–14.

51. H. M. C. *De L'Isle Mss.* (London, 1966), 6:346, cited in Roberts, *Schemes and Undertakings,* p. 38.

52. Robert Baillie, *The Letters and Journals of Robert Baillie,* 1: 310–11, cited in Roberts, *Schemes and Undertakings,* p. 47.

53. St. John, "Speech Concerning Ship Money," p. 22. For an extended discussion of the legal arguments, see W. G. Palmer, "Oliver St. John and the Legal Language of Revolution, *The Historian* 51 (February 1989): 263–82.

54. Fletcher, *Outbreak of the Civil War;* Caroline Hibbard, *Charles I and the Popish Plot* (Chapel Hill, N.C., 1983); and Morrill, "The Religious Context of the Civil War." For a different point of view, see Martin J. Havran, *The Catholics of Caroline England* (Stanford, 1962).

55. The best discussion of St. John's religious beliefs may be found in Valerie Pearl, "Oliver St. John and the Middle Group in the Long Parliament: August 1643–May 1644," *English Historical Review* 81 (1966): 490–519.

56. Notestein, *D'Ewes,* p. 489.

57. B. L. Add. Mss. 25285, 25278. It should be added that the commonplace book is of limited value in assessing St. John's religious beliefs because it is not clear how much of it represents his thought and how much was written by other members of his family.

58. Clarendon, *History,* 1: 229–33; B. L. Add. Mss. 4180, fol. 170v. Clarendon reported that "they" (presumably including Pym) endeavored to "make the severity and rigour of the House as formidable as possible and to make as many men

apprehend themselves obnoxious to the House. . . . When they had sufficiently startled men by these proceedings . . . they rested satisfied . . . without making haste to proceed against either things or persons being willing to keep men in suspense. For this reason they used their skill to keep off any debate of Ship Money, that the whole business might hang like a meteor over the heads of those that were in any degree faulty in it; and it was observable, when, notwithstanding all their diversions, that business was brought into debate and upon that (which could not be avoided) the Lord Finch named as an avowed factor and procurer of that odious judgement. . . ." Because St. John attacked Finch and Ship Money with feverish persistence, we may assume that he was opposed to Pym's diversionary tactics.

Sir Edward Nicholas stated that, as a result of his efforts to save Finch, Pym was "reported in the town to be grown cold in the business of the commonwealth." See also Clayton Roberts, *The Growth of Responsible Government in England* (Cambridge, 1966), pp. 78–79, n. 2; and Jones, *Politics and the Bench* (New York, 1971), p. 139.

59. Notestein, *D'Ewes*, pp. 75–76.

60. B.L. Thomason, E 200(4); B.L. Harl. Mss. 163, fol. 312.

61. Clarendon, *History*, 1: 245; Fletcher, *Outbreak of the Civil War*, pp. 100–101.

62. John Rushworth, *The Tryal of Thomas, Earl of Strafford* (London, 1680), p. 72. The entire charge may be found on pp. 61–75. Perhaps the most-puzzling episode in St. John's career concerns his appointment as the King's Solicitor on 29 January 1641. According to Clarendon (*History*, 1: 280–81), the earl of Bedford prevailed on the king to appoint St. John and others to high offices in government as part of a larger compromise to save Strafford. For a detailed study of Bedford's undertaking, see Clayton Roberts, "The Earl of Bedford and the Coming of the English Revolution," *Journal of Modern History* 49 (December 1977): 600–616. Bedford, of course, had been St. John's close associate since 1629 (see Clarendon, *History* 1: 246–47), as well as his political patron. But if either Bedford or Charles hoped that the appointment would deter St. John from pursuit of Strafford, he was badly mistaken.

63. Strafford's trial has, of course, sparked a controversy among historians. C. V. Wedgwood, in her biography of Strafford (see n. 4), argued that Pym and his associates manufactured a new theory of treason to secure Strafford's execution. This thesis has been subjected to several revisions, particularly by Conrad Russell, "The Theory of Treason in the Trial of Strafford," *English Historical Review* 80 (1965): 30–50; and J. H. Timmis, "Evidence and 1 Elizabeth I, Cap. 6; The Basis of the Lord's Decision in the Trial of Strafford," *Historical Journal* 21 (1978): 677–83.

To my mind the most lucid and convincing discussion of the subject may be found in W. R. Stacey, "Matter of Fact, Matter of Law, and the Attainder of the Earl of Strafford," *American Journal of Legal History* 29 (October 1985): 323–48. I am grateful to Professor Stacey for allowing me to read a copy of his paper in advance of its publication and for an instructive discussion of the subject.

64. On the importance of the two-witness rule, see Wedgwood, *Strafford*, pp. 301–5, 311–12; Stacey, "Matter of Fact, Matter of Law," pp. 328–29.

65. Robert Baillie, *Letters and Journals*, 1: 330.

66. Evidence of Pym's initial opposition to attainder may be found in B.L. Harl. Mss. 163, fols. 47–48a; B.L. Harl. Mss. 164, fols. 165a, 165b.

67. B.L. Harl. Mss. 163, fols. 27r, 28r, 43–53r. See also Perez Zagorin, *The Court and the Country* (New York, 1969), pp. 220–22.

68. B.L. Harl. Mss. 163, fol. 45. D'Ewes was "amazed to see so many speak on

Strafford's side." See also Rushworth, *Tryal of Strafford*, pp. 50–53.

69. H.M.C., Cowper Mss. (London, 1888), 2:279; B.L. Harl. Mss. 476, fol. 180r.

70. B.L. Harl, Mss. 476, fol. 598b. We can only speculate on St. John's reasons for supporting attainder over impeachment. St. John was a member of the committee that prepared the case against Strafford (*C.J.*, 2: 26–27). So he had undoubtedly examined the available evidence. As we have seen, he had devoted much attention to treson theory. Yet, we also know that he supported attainder from an early date, and he did not participate in the impeachment proceedings, which were conducted principally by Pym, Glynn, Maynard, and Whitelocke. St. John did try to prevent Strafford from using counsel, and he tried to have the bishops excluded from the proceedings. (See Notestein, *D'Ewes*, p. 468.) St. John's absence from the trial is curious. Was he deliberately excluded from the prosecution team? Was he a poor trial lawyer? Did he avoid the impeachment proceedings because he had discerned the problem of the two-witness rule and concluded that impeachment would fail?

71. St. John, "An Argument of Law Concerning the Bill of Attainder of High Treason of Thomas, Earl of Strafford," B. L. Thomason, E 208 (7), p. 6.

72. Ibid., pp. 5–8.

73. Ibid., pp. 9–10.

74. Ibid., pp. 25–27.

75. Ibid., p. 63.

76. Ibid., p. 64.

77. Ibid., p. 65.

78. Ibid., p. 72.

79. Ibid. D'Ewes (B.L. Harl. Mss. 164, fol. 193r) reported that St. John's "learned argument" gave "high satisfaction to all men gradually." But he added that Strafford, at the conclusion of the speech, exclaimed, "What, is this all he can say?"

Chapter 3. Rendering to Caesar and Parliament

1. *C.S.P., Domestic*, (1640–41), Charles I, 17: 584.

2. See especially Anthony Fletcher, *The Outbreak of the English Civil War* (New York, 1981); and Perez Zagorin, *The Court and the Country* (New York, 1969); Sheila Lambert, "The Opening of the Long Parliament," *Historical Journal* 27, no. 2 (1984): 265–87; John Morrill, "The Religious Context of the English Civil War," *Transactions of the Royal Historical Society*, 5th ser., vol. 34 (1984): 155–78.

3. Clarendon, *History*, 1: 320–21.

4. H.M.C., Portland Mss., 1: 12; *C.S.P., Venetian* (London, 1900–40), 1640–42, pp. 141–42, 147, 149.

5. Charles Carlton, *Charles I: The Personal Monarch* (London, 1983), p. 225.

6. The tense atmosphere of early May is described in Zagorin, *The Court and the Country*, pp. 222–26; and Caroline Hibbard, *Charles I and the Popish Plot* (Chapel Hill, N.C., 1983), pp. 193–96.

7. Lambert, "Opening of Long Parliament," p. 281.

8. B.L. Thomason Tracts, E 208 (7), p. 71.

9. Kevin Sharpe, "Crown, Parliament, and Locality: Government and Community in Early Stuart England," *English Historical Review* 397 (April 1986), p. 348.

10. For details, see Hibbard, *Charles and the Popish Plot*, pp. 193–96.

11. Anthony Fletcher gives an astute summary of Pym's activities in the early stages of the Long Parliament. See *Outbreak of the Civil War*, pp. 34–41.

12. See chapter 2 for St. John's attitudes towards attainder.

13. B.L. Harl. Mss. 164, fol. 193r.

14. Robert Baillie, *The Letters and Journals of Robert Baillie* (Edinburgh, 1841–42), 1: 349–50.

15. John Nalson, *An Impartial Collection* (London, 1862–83), 2: 237.

16. See chapter 2 for an extended discussion of the differences between Pym and St. John.

17. Conrad Russell, "The Parliamentary Career of John Pym, 1621–29," in Clark, Smith, and Tyacke, eds., *The English Commonwealth, 1547–1640* (New York, 1979), p. 148.

18. Ibid., p. 149.

19. Clarendon, *History,* 1: 245–47.

20. B.L. Thomason Tracts, E 208 (7), p. 72.

21. For some examples of St. John's clashes with other members, including Pym and Hampden, see E. S. Cope, ed., *Proceedings in the Short Parliament of 1640,* Camden Society, 4th ser., vol. 19 (London, 1977), p. 209; Wallace Notestein, ed., *The Journal of Sir Symonds D'Ewes from the Beginning of the Long Parliament to the Opening of the Trial of the Earl of Strafford* (New Haven, 1923), pp. 75–76; and Maija Jansson, ed., *Two Diaries of the Long Parliament* (New York, 1984), p. 7.

22. B.L. Harl. 163, fols. 616a–617b, 638a, 640a. See also the discussion in Clayton Roberts, *Schemes and Undertakings: A Study of English Politics in the Seventeenth Century* (Columbus, 1985), p. 50; and Russell, "Parliament and the King's Finances," in Russell, ed., *The Origins of the English Civil War* (London, 1973), pp. 91–118, especially pp. 114–16.

23. B.L. Harl. Mss. 163, fols. 243v, 256. See Roberts *Schemes and Undertakings,* p. 50.

24. Fletcher, *Outbreak of the Civil War,* p. 28.

25. Clarendon, *History,* 1: 281.

26. B.L. Harl. Mss., 163, fol. 121a. See also James C. Spalding and Maynard F. Brass, "Reduction of Episcopacy as a Means to Unity in England, 1640–42," *Church History* 30 (1961): 414–32.

27. For an interesting discussion of this point, see Michael Mendle, *Dangerous Positions: Mixed Government, the Estates of the Realm, and the Making of the Answer to the XIX Propositions* (Tuscaloosa, 1985), pp. 155–62.

28. Clarendon, *History,* 1: 314–15.

29. S. R. Gardiner, ed., *Documents Relating to the Proceedings Against William Prynne in 1634 and 1637* (London, 1876), pp. 77–78; E. S. Cope, *Proceedings in the Short Parliament of 1640,* p. 168.

30. Compare, for example, his speech on the bishops, found in B.L. Thomason Tracts, E 200 (24), with the Ship Money speech, B.L. Thomason Tracts, E 196 (1) both delivered at approximately the same time. For St. John's lack of participation in the February debates, see Notestein, *D'Ewes,* pp. 306–51, although both Pym and St. John supported it. (See pp. 337–38, no. 20.)

31. Clarendon, *History,* 1: 308. See also the discussion of Bedford in this work, pp. 22, 74, 80.

32. Fletcher, *Outbreak of the Civil War,* p. 106; B.L. Harl. Mss. 163, fol. 312; B.L. Harl. Mss. 164, fols. 217–217v.

33. Fletcher, *Outbreaks of the Civil War,* pp. 100–1.

34. Robert Baillie, *Unlawfulness and Danger in Limited Episcopacy* (1641), pp. 19, 27; cited in Mendle, *Dangerous Positions,* p. 145, n. 27.

35. C. V. Wedgwood, *The King's Peace, 1637–1641* (New York, 1955), pp. 434–35.

36. Clarendon, *History,* 1: 365–66.

37. B. L. Harl. Mss. 165, fol. 223r.

38. W. G. Palmer, "Invitation to a Beheading: Factions in Parliament, the Scots, and the Execution of Archbishop William Laud in 1645," *Historical Magazine of the Protestant Episcopal Church* 12, no. 1 (March 1983): 17–27.

39. B.L. Harl. Mss. 163, fol. 285.

40. B.L. Harl. Mss. 163, fol. 344b.

41. Diary of Thomas Peyton (transcript at the Yale Center for Parliamentary History), 6/30, fol. 137.

42. B.L. Harl. Mss. 163, fol. 382b.

43. Clarendon, *History,* 1: 281. (See note 25 above.)

44. B.L. Harl. Mss. 163, fol. 299.

45. B.L. Harl. Mss. 163, fol. 329a.

46. Gardiner, *Constitutional Documents,* pp. 163–66.

47. Derek Hirst, *Authority and Conflict: England, 1603–1658* (Cambridge, Mass., 1986), p. 206.

Chapter 4. The Coming of the Civil War

1. *Statues of the Realm,* 5: 104–5. For other limited grants, see Idem., 114–15, 132–33, 135–37.

2. B.L. Harl. Mss. 164, fols. 1b, 11a; B.L. Harl. 5047, fol. 60a.

3. Conrad Russell, "England's Last Poll Tax," *History Today* 37 (October 1987): 9–11.

4. *C.J.,* 2: 241.

5. B.L. Harl. Mss. 164, fols. 107b–108a.

6. Quoted in Derek Hirst, *Authority and Conflict: England, 1603–1658* (Cambridge, Mass., 1986), p. 208.

7. Historical Manuscripts Commission, *Salisbury Mss.,* 24: 277.

8. Willson H. Coates, ed., *The Journal of Sir Simonds D'Ewes from the First Recess of the Long Parliament to the withdrawal of King Charles from London* (New Haven, 1942), pp. 27, 43. See also Michael Mendle, *Dangerous Positions: Mixed Government, the Estates of the Realm and the Answer to the XIX Propositions* (Tuscaloosa, 1985), p. 162. Mendle argues that St. John erred in his insistence that bishops were not a "third estate and degree" while at the same time conceding that the bishops were nobles.

9. See the discussion in Anthony Fletcher, *The Outbreak of the English Civil War* (New York, 1981), pp. 136–38.

10. Coates, *D'Ewes,* p. 94.

11. Ibid.

12. *C.J.,* 2: 25.

13. Coates, *D'Ewes,* pp. 183–86.

14. Ibid., p. 125–26.

15. Ibid., p. 196–7.

16. Ibid., p. 202.

17. Ibid., pp. 216–17.

18. Ibid., p. 244; Clarendon, *History,* 1: 365–66.

19. Clarendon, *History,* 1: 445–46.

20. Ibid., p. 440.

21. See the discussion in Fletcher, *Outbreak of the Civil War,* pp. 172–78. Coke is quoted by Fletcher on p. 177. On the bishops' impeachment, see Mendle, *Dangerous*

Positions, p. 165. In effect, the Commons used Williams and the bishops who sided with him as hostages. After the king signed the Exclusion Bill, Parliament released the bishops and took no further action on the impeachment.

22. Ibid., p. 229.

23. For breach of privilege, see Willson H. Coates, Anne Steele Young, and Vernon F. Snow, *The Private Journals of the Long Parliament* (New Haven, 1982), pp. 4–61. For Charles, see Fletcher, *Outbreak of the Civil War,* p. 413.

24. Coates, Young, Snow, *Private Journals,* p. 34. See also B.L. Harl. Mss. 163, fol. 6.

25. Coates, Young, and Snow, *Private Journals,* p. 83. It should also be mentioned that, in May 1641, St. John had blasted those who defended the Army Plotters on the grounds that they were acting in the service of the Crown. See B.L., Sloane Mss. 3317, fol. 29.

26. Coates, Young, and Snow, *Private Journals,* p. 96.

27. Ibid., p. 111.

28. Ibid., p. 176.

29. Ibid., p. 177.

30. Ibid.

31. Perez Zagorin, *The Court and the Country* (New York, 1969), pp. 299–301.

32. Ibid., pp. 301–3.

33. Gardiner, *Constitutional Documents,* pp. 245–47.

34. For the absence of strong commentary from St. John, see the *Private Journals* for March. For his only recorded support of the Militia Bill, see Bulstrode White-locke, *Memorials of the English Affairs* (Oxford, 1853), 1: 165.

35. Coates, Young, and Snow, *Private Journals,* pp. 424, 433.

36. "A Remonstrance or Declaration of Parliament," B. L. Thomason Tracts, E 148 (23).

37. Gardiner, *Constitutional Documents,* p. 257.

38. Clarendon, *History,* 2: 109–19; Coates, Young, and Snow, *Private Journal,* p. 367; *C.S.P., Venetian,* p. 169; *L.J.,* 6: 305, 18; Richard Greaves and Robert Zaller, eds., *Biographical Dictionary of British Radicals in the Seventeenth Century* (Brighton, Sussex, 1984), 3: 129.

39. B.L. Add. Mss. 14827, fol. 123; *C.J.,* 2: 600.

40. B.L. Harl. Mss. 163, fol. 312.

41. Ibid.

42. B.L. Add. Mss. 18777, fols. 114v–115. This episode is discussed in Valerie Pearl, "The 'Royal Independents' in the English Civil War," *Transactions of the Royal Historical Society,* 5th ser. vol. 18 (1968): 79–80.

43. See chapters 5–8 for an extensive discussion of the problems between St. John and Holles.

44. B.L. Harl. Mss. 164, fol. 275; *C.J.,* 2: 906, 928.

45. See especially Anthony Fletcher, "The Coming of the War," in John Morrill, ed., *Reactions to the English Civil War* (New York, 1982), pp. 29–49; John Morrill, "The Religious Context of the English Civil War," *Transactions of the Royal Historical Society,* 5th ser. vol. 34 (1984): 168–71.

Chapter 5. The Reign of King St. John

1. J. H. Hexter, *The Reign of King Pym* (Cambridge, Mass., 1941).

2. Ibid., pp. 160–65.

3. Valerie Pearl, "Oliver St. John and the Middle Group in the Long Parliament: August 1643–May 1644," *English Historical Review* 81 (1966): 490–519. David Underdown's *Pride's Purge: Politics in the Puritan Revolution* (Oxford, 1971) is another work written in the tradition of *The Reign of King Pym*. Two dissenting views should be noted. See Lotte Glow, "Political Affiliations in the House of Commons after Pym's Death," *Bulletin of the Institute of Historical Research* 38 (1965): 48–70; and J. R. MacCormack, *Revolutionary Politics in the Long Parliament* (Cambridge, Mass., 1973).

4. S. R. Gardiner, *Constitutional Documents,* pp. 267–73. The Scots' role is considered in Lawrence Kaplan, *Politics and Religion during the English Revolution* (New York, 1976).

5. Pearl, "St. John and the Middle Group," p. 499.

6. Robert Baillie, *The Letters and Journals of Robert Baillie,* 3 vols. (Edinburgh, 1841–42), 2: 133; *Mercurius Britannicus,* 11 January 1644, B.L. Thomason, E 81 (20), p. 154.

7. *Four Speeches Delivered at Guildhall . . . 6 October 1643,* B.L. Thomason, E 388 (1). See also *The Parliament Scout,* B.L. Thomason, E 70 (23).

8. B.L. Harl. Mss. 165, fols. 162–162v.

9. Kaplan, *Politics and Religion,* p. xx.

10. Patricia Crawford, *Denzil Holles; A Study of His Political Career* (London, 1979), p. 107.

11. Ibid.

12. Ibid., 37–39, 49–52; B.L. Harl. Mss. 163, fols. 247v, 256. See also chapter 3 for details.

13. Clive Holmes, *The Eastern Association and the English Civil War* (Cambridge, 1974), p. 178.

14. Details on Essex's life and career may be found in Vernon F. Snow, *Essex the Rebel: The Life of Robert Devereaux, 1591–1646* (Lincoln, Neb., 1970).

15. B.L. Harl. Mss. 164, fol. 243.

16. Ibid., fol. 223r.

17. Ibid., fols. 2661, 2661b.

18. Ibid., fols. 2284–230; *C.J.,* 3: 370. In the end the matter was referred to a committee, and Holland was acquitted.

19. Baillie, *Letters,* 2: 136.

20. B.L. Harl. Mss. 165, fols. 266a, 266b.

21. C. V. Wedgwood, *The King's War, 1641–1647* (London, 1958), p. 293. The composition of the Committee of Both Kingdoms has been analyzed by Hexter in "The Rise of the Independent Party" (Harvard University Ph.D. thesis, 1936). Hexter concluded that the membership of the committee could not be considered hostile to Essex. Moreover, the exclusion of Denzil Holles from the committee was probably a procedural rather than a partisan move. People with known prejudices on certain issues, as Holles had against Essex, were often excluded from the committee considering that particular issue. This circumstances often caused members to refrain from speaking on the particular issue they opposed so that they could get placed on the committee considering it and kill it quickly behind the scenes. (I am grateful to Mark Kishlansky for pointing out this practice to me.) Nevertheless, it can still be maintained that the establishment of the Committee of Both Kingdoms had unpleasant consequences for Essex. Even after its modification, Essex, Holles, and Stapleton remained adamantly opposed to it.

22. Clarendon, *History,* 3: 508.

23. See the excellent discussion of St. John's religious beliefs in Pearl, "St. John and the Middle Group," 500–501.

24. B.L. Harl. Mss. 163, fol. 154b.

25. Denzil Holles, *Memoirs,* in Francis Maseres, ed., *Select Tracts on the English Civil Wars* (London, 1813), p. 191.

26. *C.S.P. Venetian,* 1643–37, p. 162.

27. John Bruce, ed., *The Quarrel between the Earl of Manchester and Oliver Cromwell* (London, 1856), pp. 72–74.

28. *C.J.,* 2: 626.

29. Baillie, *Letters and Journals,* 2: 230; see also Crawford, *Holles,* p. 106.

30. B.L. Add. Mss. 5640, fols. 349–50.

31. Bulstrode Whitelocke, *Memorials of the English Affairs,* 4 vols. (Oxford, 1853), 2: 343–47.

32. Thomas Hill, "The Season for England's Self-Reflection," B.L. Thomason, E 6 (3); cited in Mark Kishlansky, *The Rise of the New Model Army* (Cambridge, 1979), p. 26.

33. *C.S.P. Domestic,* 1644–45, p. 148.

34. Authorship of the Self-Denying Ordinance remains a mystery. Most historians believe that Vane was the man behind it. (See Wedgwood, *The King's War,* p. 390). As Hexter wrote in his unpublished dissertation "The Rise of the Independent Party" (Harvard University, Ph.D. diss., 1936), "to bamboozle a faction is a real feat; Vane bamboozled a nation" (p. 340). However, the close connection between St. John and Vane, observed by contemporaries on almost every matter of importance, 1643–44 (the Solemn League and Covenant, the Holland Affair, the establishment of the Committee of Both Kingdoms), makes it more likely that the two acted in conjunction. As we have seen, St. John rarely made controversial motions himself, even when he was the author of them.

35. B.L. Harl. Mss. 166, fol. 194; B.L. Add. Mss. 31116, fol. 200b.

36. W. C. Abbott, ed., *The Writings and Speeches of Oliver Cromwell* (Cambridge, Mass., 1937–47), 1: 314–15.

37. Baillie, *Letters and Journals,* 2: 247; *The Scottish Dove,* 13 December 1644; B.L. Thomason, E 27 (7).

38. In his *The Rise of the New Model Army,* Mark Kishlansky has offered an important and provocative argument regarding the creation of the Army on principles of consensus and moderation. Kishlansky shows that the New Model was not a radical departure from previous armies and that it in many respects was a compromise between factions. I hope that it is possible to agree and disagree with his interpretation. Clearly Kishlansky has shown the elements of compromise in the Army's creation. On the other hand, principles of compromise may be followed but for radical ends. St. John and Vane pursued consensus decision making not because they were trying to make everyone happy, but because it was the only way to implement their solution to the Army's problems.

39. Whitelocke, *Memorials,* 2: 349. For the opposition of Holles and the peace party, see Clarendon, *History,* 3: 508.

40. B.L. Add. Mss. 31116, fol. 179a.

41. Kaplan, *Politics and Religion,* pp. 92, 97.

42. H. R. Trevor-Roper, *Archbishop Laud* (London, 1961), p. 410.

43. T. B. Howell, *State Trials* (London, 1809–29), 4: 599.

44. "A Brief Relation of the Death and Sufferings of the Archbishop of Canterbury," B.L. Thomason, E 269 (20); and "The Life and Death of William Laud, Archbishop of Canterbury," B.L. Thomason, E 26 (17).

45. Sabran is cited in Kaplan, *Politics and Religion,* p. 100; *Mercurius Aulicus,* 11 January 1645; B. L. Thomason, E 27 (7). Others who believed that Laud's execution was for the Scots' benefit include the anonymous author of "A Brief Relation of the

Death and Sufferings of the Archbishop of Canterbury," B. L. Thomason, E 269 (20), and Thomas Hobbes, "Behemoth," in *Works,* ed. William Molesworth (New York, 1963), 6: 165.

46. Sabran to Brienne, 30 January 1645, Public Record Office, 31/3/75, fol. 76v.

47. B.L.. Add. Mss. 31116, fol. 179a.

48. Clarendon, *History of the Rebellion,* 3: 492.

49. B.L. Harl. Mss. 166, fol. 250b; B. L. Add. Mss. 18780, fols. 123a, 124b. It should be noted that a parliamentary ordinance of 19 August 1645 established a Presbyterian Church structure, which, however, was never implemented. Nor was the ordinance ever repealed under the Commonwealth or the Protectorate. See C. H. Firth and R. S. Rait, eds., *Acts and Ordinances of the Interregnum, 1642–1660,* 3 vols. (London, His Majesty's Stationary Office, 1911), 1: 749–54.

Chapter 6. Against the Current: St. John and Holles's Ascendancy

1. Robert Baillie, *The Letters and Journals of Robert Baillie,* 3 vols. (Edinburgh, 1841–42), 2: 230.

2. *Mercurius Aulicus,* 23 February–2 March 1645, B.L. Thomason, E 272 (13).

3. For the Scots' continuing inability to grasp English resentment of them, see Lawrence Kaplan, *Politics and Religion during the English Revolution: The Scots and the Long Parliament, 1643–45* (New York: 1976); Baillie, *Letters and Journals,* 2: 265–66.

4. B.L. Harl. Mss. 165, fol. 249b; B.L. Add. 18799, fol. 34b. For other indications of St. John's city connections, see B.L. Harl. Mss. 165, fols. 251; B.L. Harl. Mss. 166, fol. 4b; B.L. Add. Mss. 31116, fol. 83.

5. Baillie, *Letters and Journals,* 2: 133.

6. B.L. Thomason, E 29 (3); E 30 (2).

7. B.L. Harl. Mss. 166, fol. 23b; *C.J.,* 4: 415, 458, 468, 485.

8. Baillie, *Letters and Journals,* 2: 279.

9. Conversely, some in Parliament thought that it was an Independent Plot against Cranford. See B.L. Harl. Mss. 166, fol. 218r.

10. *Manifest Truths,* B.L. E 343 (1), p. 69.

11. *C.J.,* 4: 212–13.

12. Baillie, *Letters and Journals,* 2: 487–89; B.L. Harl. Mss. 166, fol. 219. The oddities about the subcommittee were discovered by Violet Rowe, *Sir Henry Vane the Younger* (London, 1970), p. 68, n. 1.

13. For a recent examination of the Savile Affair, see Patricia Crawford, "The Savile Affair," *English Historical Review* 90 (1975): 76–93.

14. B.L. Add. Mss. 32, 093, fol. 216.

15. Denzil Holles, *Memoirs of Denzil, Lord Holles,* p. 213, in F. Maseres, ed., *Select Tracts Relating to the Civil Wars in England,* 2 vols. (London, 1815).

16. B.L. Add. Mss. 32093, fol. 216.

17. Holles, *Memoirs,* pp. 212–14.

18. B.L. Add. Mss. 37343, fols. 357v–400.

19. B.L. Add. Mss. 31116, fol. 25.

20. B.L. Add. Mss. 37343, fols. 357v–400.

21. In 1644 during the Holland debates St. John had used Browne to do his dirty work. (See B.L. Harl. Mss. 165, fol. 223r, and chapter 5 of this work.)

22. Bulstrode Whitelocke, *Memorials of the English Affairs,* 4 vols. (London, 1853), 2: 462.

23. Crawford, "The Savile Affair," p. 91.

24. The disintegration of St. John's reputation was not immediately visible in 1645, but the Savile Affair was probably important in explaining the depths to which St. John sank in 1647.

25. Clarendon, *History of the Rebellion* 8: 248; Holles, *Memoirs,* p. 202.

26. J. H. Hexter, *Reappraisals in History,* 2d ed. (Chicago, 1979), pp. 219–40.

27. There is also abundant post-Hexter literature on this question. See particularly the debates between George Yule and David Underdown. See also George Yule, *The Independents in the English Civil War* (Cambridge, 1958); idem, "Independents and Revolutionaries," *Journal of British Studies* 7 (1968): 11–32; David Underdown, "The Independents Reconsidered," *Journal of British Studies* 3 (1964): 57–84, idem, "The Independents Again," *Journal of British Studies* 8 (1968): 94–118. For Holles as an Erastian, see Patricia Crawford, *Denzil Holles, 1598–1680: A Study of His Political Career* (London, 1979), p. 123.

28. Valerie Pearl, " 'The Royal Independents' in the English Civil War," *Transactions of the Royal Historical Society,* 5th ser., vol. 18 (1968): 69–96.

29. Margaret F. Steig, ed., *The Diary of John Harington, M.P., 1646–53* (Old Woking, Surrey, 1977), pp. 79–81. (Hereafter, this work is cited as *Diary of John Harington*).

30. The complexity of the groups is stressed in most of the best recent monographs. See especially David Underdown, *Pride's Purge: Politics in the Puritan Revolution* (Oxford, 1971), pp. 45–75; J. R. MacCormack, *Revolutionary Politics in the Long Parliament* (Cambridge, Mass., 1973), pp. 327–46; Crawford, *Holles,* pp. 100–103; and, finally, Valerie Pearl, "Oliver St. John and the Middle Group in the Long Parliament, August 1643–May 1644," *EHR,* 81 (1966): 490–519.

31. *Vindiciae Veritatis,* p. 6; cited in Underdown, *Pride's Purge,* pp. 62–63.

32. Mark A. Kishlansky, *The Rise of the New Model Army* (Cambridge, 1979), pp. 139–42; David Underdown, "Party Management in Recruiter Elections, 1645–48," *EHR* 83 (1968): 235–64.

33. Baillie, *Letters and Journals,* 2: 365–68.

34. Harington, *Diary of John Harington,* p. 26.

35. Ibid.

36. B.L. Add. Mss. 31116, fol. 269a; *C.J.,* 4: 545, 552.

37. Holles's aims are discussed in Kishlansky, *The New Model Army,* pp. 160–64; Crawford, *Holles,* pp. 139–42.

38. Derek Hirst, *Authority and Conflict,* p. 267.

39. *C.J.,* 4: 467; B.L. Add. Mss. 33116, fol. 258v; *L.J.,* 8: 202. See the discussion in Crawford, *Holles,* p. 124. It should be noted that a few months earlier, in September 1645, St. John had bitterly attacked a petition accusing the Commons of failing to deal sincerely with Presbyterianism. A committee, said St. John, should be formed to investigate the authors of the petition. See B.L. Add. Mss. 18780, fols. 123a, 124b.

40. Baillie, *Letters and Journals,* 2: 362.

41. *Weekly Intelligencer,* 4–11 August 1646, B. L. Thomason E 358 (8); *A Warning to All the Inhabitants of London,* B.L. E 328 (24); cited in Rowe, *Vane the Younger,* p. 86.

42. S. R. Gardiner, *Constitutional Documents of the Puritan Revolution, 1625–1660* (Oxford, 1906), pp. 290–306.

43. J. G. Fotheringham, ed., *The Diplomatic Correspondence of Jean De Montreuil and the Brothers De Bellievre: French Ambassadors in England and Scotland, 1645–1648* (Edinburgh, 1898), 1: 280.

44. B.L. Harl. Mss. 166, fol. 193; cited in Rowe, *Vane the Younger,* p. 90, n. 1.

45. Rowe, *Vane the Younger*, pp. 90–91.

46. John Lilburne, *Jonah's Cry Out of the Whale's Belly*, B. L. Thomason E 400 (5), pp. 3, 12–13. For an example of Lilburne's previous support of Parliament, see *England's Birthright Justified* E 304 (17).

47. Lilburne, *Jonah's Cry*, p. 4.

48. Gardiner, *Constitutional Documents*, p. 48.

49. *C.J.*, 4: 650, 658.

50. Harington, *Diary of John Harington*, p. 34; Holles, *Memoirs*, p. 66.

51. Baillie, *Letters and Journals*, 2: 411.

52. Bodleian Library, Clarendon Mss., "Newsletter," fol. 161v.

53. Montreuil, *Correspondence*, 1: 267–68.

54. Harington, *Diary of John Harington*, p. 41–43.

55. Montreuil, *Correspondence*, 1: 280.

56. Harington, *Diary of John Harington*, p. 45.

57. *C.S.P. Venetian*, 1643–47, p. 289; cited in MacCormack, *Revolutionary Politics*, p. 146.

58. S. R. Gardiner, *History of the Great Civil War*, 3 vols. (London, 1886–91), 2: 319; cited in Pearl, "Royal Independents," p. 70.

59. Here, I prefer the interpretation advanced in Kishlansky, *The New Model Army*, pp. 277–84, over that in MacCormack, *Revolutionary Politics*, pp. 309–12.

Chapter 7. Decline and Disillusion

1. Bodleian Library, Clarendon Mss., "Letter of Intelligence," 11 April 1647, fol. 165.

2. H.M.C. *Portland MS.*, 1: 447–48.

3. Denzil Holles, *Memoirs of Denzil, Lord Holles*, in Francis Maseres, ed., *Select Tracts Relating to the Civil Wars in England*, 2 vols. (London, 1815), 1: 189.

4. Ibid., 1: 209.

5. William Dugdale, *The Life, Diary, and Correspondence*, ed. W. Hamper (London, 1827), pp. 300–303; cited in J. R. MacCormack, *Revolutionary Politics in the Long Parliament* (Cambridge, Mass., 1973), p. 211.

6. Patricia Crawford, *Denzil Holles: A Study of His Political Career* (London, 1979), p. 140.

7. *A Declaration of the Lords and Commons*, 30 March 1647, B. L. Thomason, E 669 (84).

8. Mark Kishlansky, *The Rise of the New Model Army*, (Cambridge, 1979), pp. xi–xii, 273–91. But see the recent argument in Austin Woolrych, *Soldiers and Statesmen: The General Council of the Army and Its Debates, 1647–1648* (Oxford, 1987), especially, pp. 19–21.

9. Ian Gentiles, "The Arrears of Pay of the Parliamentary Army at the End of the First Civil War," *Bulletin of the Institute of Historical Research* 48 (1975): 52–63.

10. Holles, *Memoirs*, p. 254.

11. *A Charge Delivered in the Name of the Army*, 30 June 1647, B. L. Thomason, E 395 (5).

12. Edmund Ludlow, *Memoirs of Edmund Ludlow*, ed. C. H. Firth (Oxford, 1894), 1: 161–62.

13. *C.J.*, 5: 259.

14. Crawford, *Holles*, pp. 158–59.

15. *The Diplomatic Correspondence of Jean Montreuil and the Brothers Bel-*

lievre, French Ambassadors in England and Scotland, 1645–48, ed. J. G. Fotheringham, 2 vols. (Edinburgh, 1898–99), 2: 18.

16. *C.J.,* 5: 44–46.

17. The increasing appearance of Haselrig and Evelyn as tellers was noted in Sir John Berkeley, "Memoirs of Sir John Berkeley," in Maseres, *Select Tracts,* 2: 471; Bodleian Library, Clarendon Mss., "Newsletter," fols. 2417, 2495. The retirement of St. John and Vane from the front lines of politics gives further credence to the important argument about the power of the nobility in J. S. A. Adamson, "The Peerage in Politics, 1645–1649" (Cambridge, Ph.D. thesis, 1986).

18. A good, circumstantial case is made for this supposition in MacCormack, *Revolutionary Politics,* pp. 161–92. Vane also absented himself. See Rowe, *Sir Henry Vane the Younger,* pp. 94–95.

19. John Lilburne, *Jonah's Cry out of the Whale's Belly,* p. 3.

20. John Wildman, *Westminster Projects,* B. L. Thomason, E 433 (15), 23 March 1648.

21. Lilburne, *Two Letters to . . . Colonel Henry Marten,* B. L. Thomason, E 407 (41), pp. 4–6.

22. *Mercurius Elenticus,* 1 March 1647–48, 8 March 1647–48, B. L. Thomason, E 431 (7), p. 6; *Mercurius Pragmaticus,* 13 June 1648–20 June 1648, B. L. Thomason, E 448 (2), p. 6.

23. Dugdale, *Life and Correspondence,* pp. 300–3. Cited in MacCormack, *Revolutionary Politics,* p. 211.

24. Gardiner, *Constitutional Documents,* pp. 316–25.

25. *The Clarke Papers,* ed. C. H. Firth, 4 vols. (London 1891–1901), 1: 231 n.

26. Wildman, *Putney Projects,* B.L. E 421 (19); S. R. Gardiner, *History of the Great Civil War,* 3 vols. (London, 1886–91), 3: 200–202.

27. D. M. Wolfe, ed., *Leveller Manifestos of the Puritan Revolution* (New York, 1967), pp. 196–222.

28. David Underdown, *Pride's Purge: Politics in the Puritan Revolution* (Oxford, 1971), p. 86. Throughout the remainder of this chapter readers will recognize my debt to this seminal work.

29. Gardiner, *Constitutional Documents,* pp. 359–70.

30. For the Putney debates, see A. S. P. Woodhouse, ed., *Puritanism and Liberty* (Chicago, 1954).

31. *C.J.,* 5: 415–16; Gardiner, *Constitutional Documents,* pp. 335–47.

32. See especially Arthur Haselrig's speech in D. E. Underdown, ed., "The Parliamentary Diary of John Boys," *Bulletin of the Institute of Historical Research* 39 (1966), p. 155.

33. *Mercurius Pragmaticus,* 11–18 April 1648, B. L. Thomason, E 435 (42), p. 2. See also *Westminster Projects, or the Mystery of Darby House,* B. L. Thomason, E 433 (15), pp. 1, 6. See also Underdown, *Pride's Purge,* p. 89.

34. Bodleian Library Ms., "Letter of Intelligence," 23 March 1648, fol. 7.

35. S. R. Gardiner, ed., *The Hamilton Papers* (London, 1880), p. 174; B.L. Add. Ms. 37344, fol. 142v; Bodleian Library, Clarendon Mss., "Letter of Intelligence," 27 April 1648, fol. 7. Cited in Underdown, *Pride's Purge,* p. 96.

36. Bodleian Library, Clarendon Mss., "Letter of Intelligence," 27 April 1648, fol. 7.

37. *C.J.,* 5: 547.

38. W. C. Abbott, ed., *The Writings and Speeches of Oliver Cromwell,* 4 vols. (Cambridge, Mass., 1937–47), 1: 644–45.

39. Underdown, *Pride's Purge,* p. 113.

40. *D.N.B.,* 17: 640–46.

41. See the discussion in St. John's post-restoration apologia, *The Case of Oliver St. John,* B. L. Thomason, E 1035 (5).

Conclusion

1. See especially the remarks of Valerie Pearl, "The 'Royal Independents' in the English Civil War," *Transactions of the Royal Historical Society,* 5th ser., vol. 18 (1969), p. 78. For fuller accounts of the period under discussion, see A. Blair Worden, *The Rump Parliament* (Cambridge, 1975), and Austin Woolrych, *Commonwealth to Protectorate* (Oxford, 1982).

2. Bulstrode Whitelocke, *Memorials of the English Affairs,* 4 vols. (London, 1853), 3: 287.

3. *C.J.,* 7: 30.

4. Whitelocke, *Memorials,* 2: 373.

5. Oliver St. John, *The Case of Oliver St. John,* B. L. Thomason, E 1035 (5), p. 6.

6. Ibid.

7. Ibid., p. 13; Samuel Pepys, *The Diary of Samuel Pepys,* eds. Robert Latham and William Matthews, 11 vols. (Berkeley, 1970–80), 1: 44–45.

8. Edmund Ludlow, *Memoirs of Edmund Ludlow,* ed. C. H. Firth, 2 vols. (London, 1894), 2: 290.

9. St. John, *The Case of Oliver St. John,* pp. 4–12.

10. John Morrill, "The Religious Context of the English Civil War," *Transactions of the Royal Historical Society,* 5th ser., vol. 34 (1984): 155–78.

11. John Bruce, ed., *The Quarrel Between the Earl of Manchester and Oliver Cromwell* (London, 1875), pp. 92–93.

12. This phrase is taken from Clayton Roberts, "The earl of Bedford and the Coming of the English Revolution," *JMH* 49 (December 1977): 600–16.

Bibliography

Manuscripts

BODLEIAN LIBRARY

1. Carte Mss.
2. Clarendon Mss., vols. 27–29
3. Tanner Mss. 88, fol. 117r

BRITISH LIBRARY

1. Additional Mss.
5640–60	Sabran's negotiations
10114	Diary of John Harington
18780	Diary of Walter Younge
18979	Fairfax Correspondence
20773	Fairfax Correspondence
31116	Diary of Laurence Whitaker
32093	Savile's Examinations
27343–45	Whitelocke's Annuls

2. Harleian Mss.
164–66	Diary of Sir Simonds D'Ewes
374	Letters of Sir Symonds D'Ewes

3. Egerton Mss. — Correspondence of Thomas Barrington

DR. WILLIAMS'S LIBRARY

1. Mss. 24, 50 — Thomas Juxon's Diary

HUNTINGDONSHIRE RECORD OFFICE

1. Manchester Mss. 19/3/2 — Land Records

PUBLIC RECORD OFFICE

1. C.O. 124 — Records of the Providence Island Company
2. 31/3/75 — Sabran Correspondence

Pamphlets and News Books

THOMASON TRACTS

University of Michigan Microfilm Series, 1971 (the pamphlets from the Thomason Collection are cited in the text by their British Library call number.)

THOMASON TRACTS (NEWS BOOKS)

The City Scout
The Complete Intelligencer
A Continuation of Certain Special and Remarkable Passages
A Diary of an Exact Journal
The Kingdom's Weekly Intelligencer
The London Post
Mercurius Aulicus
Mercurius Britannicus
Mercurius Civicus
Mercurius Militarius
The Moderate Intelligencer
The Parliamentary Scout
A Perfect Diurnal
The Scottish Dove
The True Informer

Printed Sources

Abbott, W. C., ed. *The Writings and Speeches of Oliver Cromwell.* Cambridge, Mass.: Harvard University Press, 1937–47.

Baillie, Robert. *The Letters and Journals of Robert Baillie.* 3 vols. Edinburgh, 1841–42.

Baxter, Richard. *Reliquiae Baxterianae.* Edited by M. Sylvester. London, 1693.

Bell, Robert, ed. *Memorials of the Great Civil War.* London, 1849.

Bruce, John, ed. *The Quarrel between the Earl of Manchester and Oliver Cromwell.* London: Camden Society, 1856.

Calendar of State Papers, Domestic Series, 1625–65. Edited by J. Bruce, M. A. E. Green, and W. P. Hamilton. London, 1858–97.

Calendar of State Papers, Venetian Series. Edited by A. B. Hinds. London, 1921–32.

Carte, Thomas. *A Collection of Original Letters and Papers, 1641–1648.* London, 1730.

Cary, Henry, ed. *Memorials of the Great Civil War, 1646–1652.* London, 1842.

Coates, Willson H., ed. *The Journal of Sir Simonds D'Ewes from the First Recess of the Long Parliament to the withdrawal of King Charles from London.* New Haven: Yale University Press, 1942.

Coates, Willson H., Anne Steele Young, and Vernon F. Snow, eds. *The Private Journals of the Long Parliament.* New Haven: Yale University Press, 1982.

Cole, Maia Jansson, ed. *Two Diaries of the Long Parliament*. New York: St. Martin's Press, 1984.

Cope, E. S., ed. *Proceedings of the Short Parliament of 1640*. London: Camden Society, 1977.

Evelyn, John. *The Diary of John Evelyn*. London, 1848.

Firth, C. H., ed. *Clarke Papers*. London, Camden Society, 1891–1901.

Fotheringham, J. G., ed. *The Diplomatic Correspondence of Jean de Montreuil and the Brothers De Bellievre: French Ambassadors in England and Scotland, 1645–1648*. 2 vols. Edinburgh, 1898–89.

Gardiner, S. R., ed. *Constitutional Documents of the Puritan Revolution, 1625–1649*. Oxford: Clarendon Press, 1889.

———. *Documents Relating to the Proceedings against William Prynne in 1634 and 1637*. London: Camden Society, 1876.

———. *The Hamilton Papers*. London: Camden Society, 1880.

Haller, William, and Godfrey Davies, eds. *The Leveller Tracts*. New York: Columbia University Press, 1944.

Halliwell, J. E. *The Autobiography and Correspondence of Sir D'Ewes*. 2 vols. London, 1845.

Historical Manuscripts Commission. 7th Report, Lowndes Mss. 8th Report, Manchester Mss. 11th Report, Hamilton Mss.

Howell, T. B. *State Trials*. London, 1816.

Hutchinson, Lucy. *Memoirs of Colonel Hutchinson*. Edited by James Sutherland. Oxford: Oxford University Press, 1973.

Hyde, Edward. *History of the Rebellion*. 6 vols. Edited by W. D. MacCray. Oxford, 1888.

Journals of the House of Commons, 1640–1666. London, 1803.

Journals of the House of Lords, 1628–1666. London, n.d.

Kearney, Hugh. *The Eleven Years' Tyranny of Charles I*. London: Historical Association, 1962.

Laing, David, ed. *The Letters and Journals of Robert Baillie*. Edinburgh, 1841–43.

Laud, William. *The Works of William Laud*. Edited by W. Scott and J. Bliss. 7 vols. Oxford, 1847–60.

Ludlow, Edmund. *Memoirs of Edmund Ludlow*. Edited by C. H. Firth. Oxford, 1894.

Maltby, Judith, ed. *The Short Parliament Diary of Sir Thomas Aston*. London: Camden Society, 1988.

Maeseres, Francis, ed. *Select Tracts Relating to the Civil War in England*. London, 1815.

Nalson, John. *An Impartial Collection of the Great Affairs of State*. London, 1815.

Northcote, John. *The Notebook of John Northcote*. Edited by A. H. A. Hamilton. London, 1877.

Notestein, Wallace. *The Journal of Sir Simonds D'Ewes from the Beginning of the Long Parliament to the Withdrawal of King Charles from London*. New Haven: Yale University Press, 1923.

Rushworth, John. *Historical Collections*. 10 vols. London, 1712.

Snow, Vernon F., and Anne Young, eds. *The Private Journals of the Long Parliament: 7 March to 1 June 1642*. New Haven: Yale University Press, 1987.

Stieg, Margaret F., ed. *The Diary of John Harington, M.P., 1646–43.* Old Woking, Surrey: Somerset Record Society Publications, 1977.

Tibbutt, H. G., ed. *The Letter Books of Sir Samuel Luke, 1644–1645.* Bedford: Bedford Record Office, 1963.

Underdown, David, ed. "The Parliamentary Diary of John Boys." *BIHR* 39 (1966): 143–61.

Verney, Sir Ralph. *Notes of Proceedings in the Long Parliament.* Edited by J. Bruce, London: Camden Society, 1845.

———. *Verney Papers.* Edited by J. Bruce. London: Camden Society, 1845.

Waller, William. *Vindication.* London, 1793.

Whitelocke, Bulstrode. *Memorials of the English Affairs.* London, 1853.

Wolfe, D. M. *Leveller Manifestos of the Puritan Revolution.* New York: Humanities Press, 1967.

Woodhouse, A. S. P. *Puritanism and Liberty.* Chicago: University of Chicago Press, 1954.

Secondary Works (Books)

Adair, John. *A Life of John Hampden: The Patriot.* London: Weidenfield and Nelson, 1975.

Adams, H. F., and J. F. Folland. *The Life and Times of Sir Harry Vane the Younger.* Boston: Gambit, 1973.

Aylmer, Gerald E. *The Levellers and the English Revolution.* Ithaca: Cornell University Press, 1975.

Brunton, D., and D. H. Pennington. *The Members of the Long Parliament.* London: Allen and Unwin, 1954.

Burne, A. H., and Peter Young. *The Great Civil War.* London: Eyre and Spotiswode, 1959.

Carlton, Charles. *Archbishop William Laud.* New York: Routledge and Kegan Paul, 1987.

———. *Charles I: The Personal Monarch.* London: Routledge and Kegan Paul, 1983.

Collinson, Patrick. *The Religion of Protestants.* Oxford: Oxford University Press, 1982.

Cope, Esther S. *Politics without Parliaments, 1629–1640.* London: Allen and Unwin, 1987.

Crawford, Patricia. *Denzil Holles, 1598–1670: A Study of his Political Career.* London: Royal Historical Society, 1979.

Darby, H. C. *The Draining of the Fens.* 2d ed. Cambridge: Cambridge University Press, 1956.

Donald, Peter. *An Uncounseled King: Charles I and the Scottish Troubles, 1637–1641.* Cambridge: Cambridge University Press, 1991.

Donaldson, Gordon. *The Making of the Scottish Prayer Book of 1637.* Edinburgh: Edinburgh University Press, 1957.

Everitt, Alan. *Change in the Provinces: The Seventeenth Century.* Leicester: Leicester University Press, 1969.

———. *The Community of Kent and the Great Rebellion, 1640–1660.* Leicester: Leicester University Press, 1966.

Finlayson, Michael. *Historians, Puritanism, and the English Revolution.* Toronto: University of Toronto Press, 1983.

Firth, C. H. *Cromwell's Army.* London: Methuen, 1902.

Fletcher, Anthony. *The Outbreak of the English Civil War.* London: Edward Arnold, 1981.

Fraser, Antonia. *Cromwell: the Lord Protector.* New York: Knopf, 1973.

Gardiner, S. R. *History of England from the Accession of James I to the Outbreak of Civil War, 1603–1642.* New York: AMS Press, 1965.

———. *History of the Great Civil War.* New York: AMS Press, 1965.

George, Charles H., and Katherine George. *The Protestant Mind of the English Reformation, 1590–1640.* Princeton: Princeton University Press, 1961.

Haller, William. *The Rise of Puritanism.* New York: Columbia University Press, 1961.

Havran, Martin. *The Catholics of Caroline England.* Palo Alto, Calif.: Stanford University Press, 1962.

Hexter, J. H. *Reappraisals in History.* Evanston, Ill.: Northwestern University Press, 1961.

———. *The Reign of King Pym.* Cambridge, Mass.: Harvard University Press, 1940.

Hibbard, Caroline. *Charles I and the Popish Plot.* Chapel Hill: University of North Carolina Press, 1983.

Hill, Christopher. *Intellectual Origins of the English Revolution.* Oxford: Clarendon Press, 1965.

———. *God's Englishman.* New York: Dial Press, 1970.

———. *Puritanism and Revolution.* London: Secker and Warburg, 1958.

———. *The World Turned Upside Down.* New York: Viking, 1972.

Hirst, Derek. *Authority and Conflict: England 1603–1658.* Cambridge, Mass.: Harvard University Press, 1986.

———. *The Representative of the People? Voters and Voting in England under the Early Stuarts.* Cambridge: Cambridge University Press, 1975.

Holmes, Clive. *The Eastern Association.* Cambridge: Cambridge University Press, 1973.

Jones, W. J. *Politics and the Bench: Judges and the Origins of the English Civil War.* New York: Barnes and Noble, 1971.

Judson, Margaret. *The Crisis of the Constitution.* New Brunswick, N.J.: Rutgers University Press, 1949.

Kaplan, Lawrence. *Politics and Religion in the English Revolution.* New York: New York University Press, 1976.

Keeler, M. F. *The Long Parliament.* Philadelphia: American Philosophical Society, 1954.

Kishlansky, Mark A. *The Rise of the New Model Army.* Cambridge: Cambridge University Press, 1979.

Lamont, William. *Marginal Prynne.* London: Routledge and Kegan Paul, 1963.

Lee, Maurice. *The Road to Revolution: Scotland under Charles I.* Urbana: University of Illinois Press, 1985.

Lindley, Keith. *Fenland Riots and the English Revolution.* London: Gower, 1982.

MacCormack, J. R. *Revolutionary Politics in the Long Parliament.* Cambridge, Mass.: Harvard University Press, 1973.

MacFarlane, Alan. *The Origins of English Individualism: The Family, Property and Social Transition.* New York: Cambridge University Press, 1979.

Manning, Brian. *The English People and the English Civil War.* London: Heineman, 1976.

Manning, Brian, ed. *Religion, Politics and the English Civil War.* London: Edward Arnold, 1973.

Mason, Thomas. *Serving God and Mammon: William Juxon, 1582–1663, Bishop of London, Lord High Treasurer of England, and Archbishop of Canterbury.* Newark: University of Delaware Press, 1985.

Mendle, Michael. *Dangerous Positions: Mixed Government, the Estates of the Realm, and the Making of the Answer to the XIX Propositions.* Tuscaloosa: University of Alabama Press, 1985.

Morgan, Irvonwy. *Prince Charles' Puritan Chaplain.* London: Allen and Unwin, 1957.

Morrill, John. *The Revolt of the Provinces: Conservatives and Radicals in the English Civil War.* London: Allen and Unwin, 1976.

Newton, A. P. *The Colonizing Activities of the English Puritans.* New Haven: Yale University Press, 1932.

Parry, R. H., ed. *The English Civil War and After, 1642–1658.* London: Macmillan, 1971.

Pawlisch, Hans. *Sir John Davies and the Conquest of Ireland: A Study in Legal Imperialism.* Cambridge: Cambridge University Press, 1985.

Pearl, Valerie. *London and the Outbreak of the Puritan Revolution.* Oxford: Oxford University Press, 1960.

Pocock, J. G. A. *The Ancient Constitution and the Feudal Law.* Cambridge: Cambridge University Press, 1957.

———. *The Machiavellian Moment.* Princeton: Princeton University Press, 1975.

Prest, W. R. *The Inns of Court under Elizabeth and the Early Stuarts, 1590–1640.* London: Longman, 1972.

Rabb, Theodore K. *Enterprise and Empire: Merchant and Gentry Investment in the Expansion of England, 1575–1630.* Cambridge, Mass.: Harvard University Press, 1967.

Reeve, L. J. *Charles I and the Road to the Personal Rule.* Cambridge: Cambridge University Press, 1989.

Roberts, R. Clayton. *The Growth of Responsible Government in England.* Cambridge: Cambridge University Press, 1966.

———. *Schemes and Undertakings.* Columbus: Ohio State University Press, 1985.

Rowe, Violet. *Sir Henry Vane the Younger.* London: Athlone Press, 1970.

Russell, Conrad. *The Causes of the English Civil War.* Oxford: Oxford University Press, 1990.

Russell, Conrad, ed. *The Origins of the English Civil War.* London: Macmillan, 1973.

Solt, Leo. *Saints in Arms.* Palo Alto, Calif.: Stanford University Press, 1958.

Sommerville, J. P. *Politics and Ideology in England, 1600–1640.* London: Longman, 1986.

Spalding, Ruth. *The Improbable Puritan*. London: Faber and Faber, 1975.

Stearns, Raymond P. *The Strenuous Puritan*. Urbana: University of Illinois Press, 1954.

Stone, Lawrence. *The Causes of the English Revolution*. New York: Harper and Row, 1972.

———. *The Crisis of the Aristocracy*. Oxford: Oxford University Press, 1965.

———. *Family and Fortune: Studies in Aristocratic Finance in the Seventeenth Century*. Oxford: Oxford University Press, 1973.

———. *Family, Sex, and Marriage in England, 1500–1800*. New York: Harper and Row, 1977.

Tolmie, Murray. *The Triumph of the Saints*. Cambridge: Cambridge University Press, 1977.

Trevor-Roper, Hugh. *Archbishop Laud*. Cambridge: Cambridge University Press, 1943.

Tyacke, Nicholas. *Anti-Calvinists: The Rise of English Arminianism, c. 1590–1640* Oxford: Oxford University Press, 1987.

Underdown, David. *Pride's Purge: Politics in the Puritan Revolution*. Oxford: Oxford University Press, 1971.

———. *Revel, Riot, and Rebellion: The Problem of Popular Allegiance in the English Civil War*. Oxford: Oxford University Press, 1985.

Walzer, Michael. *The Revolution of the Saints*. New York: Atheneum, 1968.

Wedgwood, C. V. *The King's Peace*. New York: Macmillan, 1958.

———. *The King's War*. New York: Macmillan, 1959.

———. *Thomas Wentworth, the First Earl of Strafford*. London: Jonathan Cape, 1961.

Woolrych, Austin. *Soldiers and Statesmen: The General Council of the Army and its Debates, 1647–1648*. Oxford: Oxford University Press, 1987.

Worden, A. B. *The Rump Parliament*. Cambridge: Cambridge University Press, 1974.

Yule, George. *The Independents in the English Civil War*. Cambridge: Cambridge University Press, 1958.

Zagorin, Perez. *The Court and the Country*. New York: Atheneum, 1971.

Secondary Works (Articles)

Adamson, J. S. A. "The English Nobility and the Projected Settlement of 1647." *HJ* 30 (1987): 567–602.

Albright, Margaret. "The Enterprise of Fen Drainage in England under James I and Charles I: An Illustration of the Uses of Influence." *Explorations in Entrepreneurial History* 8 (1955–56): 51–65.

Christianson, Paul. "The Causes of the English Civil War: A Reappraisal." *JBS* 15 (1976): 40–75.

———. "The Peers, the People, and Parliamentary Management in the First Six Months of the Long Parliament." *JMH* 49 (1979): 575–99.

Coates, Willson S. "Some Observations on the Grand Remonstrance." *JMH* 8 (1932): 117.

Crawford, Patricia. "The Savile Affair." *EHR* 90 (1975): 76–93.

———. " 'Charles Stuart, That Man of Blood.' " *JBS* 16 (1977): 41–62.

Davies, Godfrey, "The Parliamentary Army under the Earl of Essex, 1642–5." *EHR* 49 (1934): 32–54.

Fincham, Kenneth. "The Judges' Decision on Ship Money: The Reaction of Kent." *BIHR* 57 (1984): 230–37.

Foster, Stephen. "The Presbyterian-Independents Exorcised: A Ghost Story for Historians." *Past and Present* 44 (1969): 52–75.

Gentiles, Ian. "The Arrears of Pay of the Parliamentary Army at the End of the First Civil War." *BIHR* 48 (1975): 52–63.

Glow (Mulligan), Lotte. "The Committee Men in the Long Parliament, August, 1642–December, 1643." *HJ* (1965): 1–15.

———. "The Committee of Safety." *EHR* 80 (1965): 289–313.

———. "Political Affiliations in the House of Commons after Pym's Death." *BIHR* 38 (1965): 48–70.

———. "Peace Negotiations, Politics, and the Committee of Both Kingdoms, 1644–46." *HJ* 12 (1969): 3–22.

Hexter, J. H. "The Early Stuarts and Parliament: Old Hat and *Nouvelle Vague*." *Parliamentary History* 1 (1982): 181–215.

———. "Power Struggle, Parliament, and Liberty in Early Stuart England." *MJH* 50 (1978): 1–50.

Hirst, Derek. "The Place of Principle." *Past and Present* 92 (1981): 77–99.

———. "Unanimity in the Commons, Aristocratic Intrigues, and the Origins of the English Civil War." *JMH* 50 (1978): 51–71.

Holmes, Clive. "The County Community in Early Stuart Historiography." *JBS* 19 (1980): 54–73.

Keir, D. L. "The Case of Ship Money." *Law Quarterly Review* 52 (1936): 546–74.

Kennedy, Mark E. "Charles I and Local Government: The Draining of the East and West Fens." *Albion* 15 (1983): 19–31.

Kishlansky, Mark A. "The Emergence of Adversary Politics in the Long Parliament." *JMH* 49 (1977): 617–40.

———. "The Case of the Army Truly Stated: The Creation of the New Model Army." *Past and Present* 81 (1978): 51–78.

———. "The Army and the Levellers: The Roads to Putney." *HJ* 22 (1979): 795–821.

Lambert, Sheila. "The Opening of the Long Parliament." *HJ* 27 (1984): 265–87.

Mendle, Michael. "Politics and Political Thought." In Russell, Conrad, ed. *The Origins of the English Civil War*. London: Macmillan, 1973.

Morrill, John S. "Mutiny and Discontent in the English Provincial Armies, 1645–7." *Past and Present* 56 (1972): 49–74.

———. "The Religious Context of the English Civil War." *Transactions of the Royal Historical Society*, 5th ser. vol. 34 (1984): 155–78.

Notestein, Wallace. "The Establishment of the Committee of Both Kingdoms." *American Historical Review* 17 (1912): 477–95.

Palmer, William. "Catholic Plots and the English Revolution: Some Comments." *Catholic Historical Review* 73 (1987): 81–85.

———. "Invitation to a Beheading: Factions in Parliament, the Scots, and the

Execution of Archbishop William Laud in 1645." *Historical Magazine of the Protestant Episcopal Church* 52 (1983): 17–27.

———. "Oliver St. John and the Legal Language of Revolution in England, 1640–42." *The Historian* 51 (1989): 263–81.

———. "Oliver St. John and the Middle Group in the Long Parliament, 1643–45: A Reappraisal." *Albion* 14 (1982): 20–26.

Pearl, Valerie. "Oliver St. John and the Middle Group in the Long Parliament: August, 1643–May, 1644." *EHR* 81 (1966): 499–519.

———. "The 'Royal Independents' in the English Civil War." *Transactions of the Royal Historical Society,* 5th ser., vol. 18 (1968): 69–96.

Roberts, Clayton, "The Earl of Bedford and the Coming of the English Revolution." *JMH* 49 (1977): 600–16.

Rowe, Violet. "Robert, Second Earl of Warwick and the Payment of Ship Money." *Transactions of the Essex Archaeological Society* 1 (1964–5): 160–63.

Russell, Conrad. "The British Problem and the English Civil War." *History* 72 (October 1987): 395–415.

———. "England's Last Poll Tax." *History Today* 37 (1987): 9–11.

———. "The First Army Plot of 1641." *Transactions of the Royal Historical Society,* 5 ser., vol. 38 (1988): 85–106.

———. "Land Sales, 1540–1640: A Comment on the Evidence." *Economic History Review,* 2d ser., vol. 15 (1972): 117–21.

———. "Parliament and the King's Finances." In Russell, Conrad, ed. *The Origins of the English Civil War.* London: Macmillan, 1973.

———. "Parliamentary History in Perspective." *History* 61 (1976): 1–27.

———. "The Ship Money Judgments of Bramston and Davenport." *EHR* 302 (1962): 312–18.

———. "The Theory of Treason in the Trial of Strafford." *EHR* 80 (1965): 49–53.

———. "Why Did Charles I Call the Long Parliament?" *History* 69 (1984): 375–83.

Sharpe, Kevin. "Crown, Parliament, and Locality: Government and Community in Early Stuart England." *EHR* 101 (1986): 323–50.

———. "The Personal Rule of Charles I." In Howard Tomlinson, ed. *Before the English Civil War.* New York: St. Martin's Press, 1985.

Spalding, James C., and Maynard F. Brass. "Reduction of Episcopacy as a Means to Unity in England, 1640–42." *Church History* 30 (1961): 414–32.

Stacey, W. R. "Matter of Fact, Matter of Law, and the Attainder of the Earl of Strafford." *American Journal of Legal History* 29 (October 1985): 323–48.

Timmis, J. H. "Evidence and 1 Elizabeth I, Cap. 6: The Basis of the Lords' Decision in the Trial of Strafford." *HJ* 21 (1978): 677–83.

Underdown, David E. "The Chalk and the Cheese: Contrasts among the English Clubman." *Past and Present* 85 (1979): 25–48.

———. "The Independents Reconsidered." *JBS* 3 (1964): 57–84.

———. "The Independents Again." *JBS* 8 (1968): 94–118.

———. "Party Management in Recruiter Elections, 1645–48." *EHR* 83 (1968): 235–64.

Yule, George. "Independents and Revolutionaries." *JBS* 7 (1968): 11–32.

Zagorin, Perez. "Did Strafford Change Sides?" *EHR* 101 (1986): 149–63.

Zaller, Robert. "Opposition in Early Stuart England." *Albion* (Fall 1980): 211–32.

Index